# TARGET

Thinking and
Speaking
in Primary Schools

# TARGET

# Thinking and Speaking in Primary Schools

*Essential Reading for Effective Learning*

For Class Teachers, SENCOs and Support for Learning Staff

Jeanne Reilly
and Sarah Murray

Barrington Stoke
Helen Arkell Dyslexia Centre

First published 2005 in Great Britain by Barrington Stoke Ltd,
Sandeman House, Trunk's Close, 55 High Street, Edinburgh, EH1 1SR

www.barringtonstoke.co.uk

ISBN 1-84299-158-2

Edited by Julia Rowlandson
Index by Colin Redman
Designed and typeset by GreenGate Publishing Services, Tonbridge
Printed in Spain

# Contents

# Introduction

'We have to do it independent, that means on your own.'
Jack Aged 6

'Thought is born through words.'
Vygotsky

## The aim of the book

The aim of this book is to help class teachers and learning support assistants to understand and help those children in class who have difficulty thinking and speaking.

The book gives practical ideas for teachers and assistants to use so that the children can learn more effectively. The book takes into account that different children have different learning styles and that their learning style is likely to influence how they think. So, for example, a child might learn better through what he 'sees' rather than what he 'hears'. He may prefer to think in pictures rather than words. An effective thinker will use a variety of different learning styles.

**Thinking and speaking** are two essential skills for learning and communicating. Thinking enables us to come up with the ideas we speak about. Speaking is both an important social activity as well as a vital tool for stimulating thinking in new ways.

---

For simplicity the teacher will be referred to as 'she' and the child as 'he'.

# What is thinking?

We think in order to give meaning to our experiences, to plan ahead, to be flexible, creative and reflective. Effective learners adjust their thinking and understanding of the world as they take in new information and relate it to what they already know. We think using different symbols, such as words, pictures and sounds.

Our brain sifts and sorts the information we take in through our senses. Over time, our brains become a huge filing cabinet of ideas, words and pictures which are organised together in many different ways.

Some thinking is conscious. Conscious thinking is needed for reflection and adjusting our actions. As a child matures he learns to reflect and think on his own. This 'thinking about thinking' is called **meta-cognition**. It leads to new ways of thinking.

Unconscious thinking allows us to be automatic and faster in what we do. Intuitive and creative ideas can come from unconscious thinking.

An effective learner knows when to use conscious and unconscious thought.

# What is speaking?

Speaking allows us to communicate with other people in our world. When we speak, we use words to tell others what we are thinking. Words are like the windows to our thoughts.

In order to communicate effectively, we need to know which words to use, how to put them together in sentences and how to speak in a way that fits the situation.

We also need to use the right speech sounds for the language we are speaking.

# Thinking and speaking in the classroom

When children start school, most of them are good thinkers and speakers and are ready to learn the curriculum. Being able to think and speak in large and small groups allows children to try out their thoughts and ideas. Learning requires a child to adjust their thinking.

Thinking and speaking enable the child to:

- contribute ideas to a group discussion

- organise information and plan ahead

- express ideas with precision

- sequence and analyse ideas

- put sentences together

- speak confidently and appropriately

As a child learns the curriculum, he thinks and speaks in increasingly more complex ways. Critical thinking, discussion of moral issues and creative thinking are all examples of more complex thinking.

Being able to think and speak clearly are two skills children need if they are to be able to write their ideas down clearly. Thinking, speaking and writing skills are taught alongside one another in the National Curriculum.

# Difficulties in thinking and speaking

For some children thinking and speaking do not develop easily.

Children who have problems with thinking and speaking may:

- Appear to have few ideas and produce the minimum amount of work.

- Be unable to organise their thoughts in a cohesive way so that others can understand them.

- Be unable to get their exact meaning across and use limited vocabulary.

- Only use basic sentences and vocabulary when they speak and write.

- Lack the clarity of speech expected for their age.

- Not contribute to group activities or interact with others.

Before judgements are made it is important that children's behaviour is carefully observed and described, and related to likely difficulties in thinking and speaking. For example, a child judged to be 'lazy' might, in fact, have considerable difficulty generating ideas.

Though most of the children this book can help will not have a specific diagnosis, there may be some who have been diagnosed with a 'specific learning difficulty'. The following terms might be used with these children: Specific Developmental Language Disorder, Dyslexia, Attention Deficit (Hyperactivity) Disorder, Dyspraxia, Autistic Spectrum Disorder, and Asperger's Syndrome.

This book is intended to describe rather than diagnose children's behaviour and then to offer ideas to help improve their thinking and speaking.

# How to use this book

Start with the checklists which will give you a description of what the child can do. This will help you identify any areas of need.

The checklists should point you to the relevant chapters where each skill area is described in detail. Strategies for both the teacher and child are described.

Each chapter also includes activities for teachers and assistants to use with the child. The activities should be used with a child depending on their ability and need, rather than their age.

# Areas involved in thinking and speaking

There are six skill areas which are described in this book as underpinning Thinking and Speaking. Each is covered in a separate chapter.

1   In **Thinking of Ideas** a child gives meaning to his experiences.

2   By **Organising Ideas** a child makes sense of his world as he learns new things.

3   **Finding the Right Word** allows for precise meaning to be communicated.

4   **Speaking in Sentences** allows a child to talk about complex ideas.

5   **Speaking Clearly** allows the child to be understood.

6   **Thinking and Speaking** in Conversation allows the child to share his thoughts, feelings and needs with others.

Not only do all the areas of **Thinking and Speaking** develop and interact alongside one another, but they also develop and interact with all the skills in **Listening and**

Understanding too. Below is a diagram to represent of the link between, **Thinking**, **Speaking**, **Listening and Understanding**.

Although this book focuses on **Thinking and Speaking**, it should be remembered that **Listening and Understanding** are also key skills needed for effective learning and communication.

**Target book 2, Listening and Understanding in Primary Schools** offers practical suggestions for children who need help with **Listening and Understanding**. This book should be used in parallel.

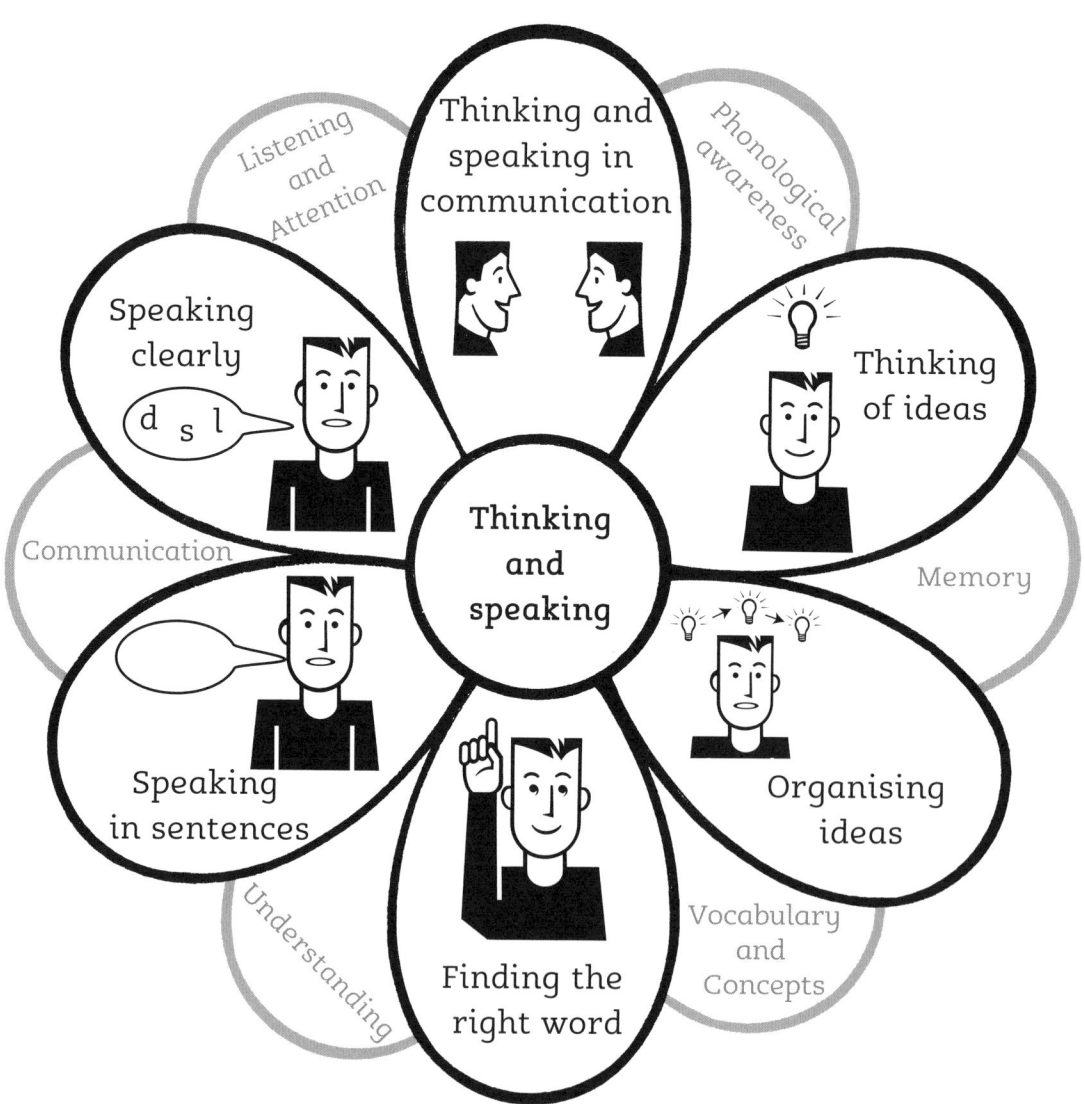

Difficulties in any one area of **Thinking and Speaking** will have repercussions on any of the other areas on the diagram. Progress in any one area will strengthen the child's learning as a whole.

# Themes throughout the book

- Effective teaching involves helping the child to think and speak. An effective teacher adapts her teaching to take account of the child's individual approach to learning.

- The most effective teachers help the child to be aware of his thinking and to understand 'how' he learns.

- A child who is aware of **how** he learns, 'meta-cognitive awareness', will be better equipped to change and adapt his thinking and be a more effective learner.

- Speaking is the bridge between thinking and writing. Children must first be able to express their ideas in spoken language before they can express them in written language. Effective teachers understand the importance of engaging children in speaking about their ideas.

- Most children need time and a quiet environment in order to think. Effective teachers allow children time to think and keep noise to a minimum when they are thinking.

- Effective teachers recognise the amount of effort a child is using in order to think and speak and will support and value what he has to say. A child experiencing difficulties in thinking and speaking is likely to be working much harder to express himself than a child who has no difficulty.

*I can't think what they're called.*

*I know what it is but just let me get it into my mind.*

*It's hard to say.*

*Weeks of the day.*

*I can't actually find it …. I lose it whenever I think of it.*

*After this day backwards one. (yesterday)*

*It's in my brain and I can't get it out.*

*Oh! How can I say it?*

*There were some words which I did understand but I couldn't describe what it was.*

*My mouth said 'juggle' when I wanted it to say 'jungle'.*

*That's a spoon when you get out of soup. (That's a soup spoon)*

# Checklists

## Identifying what the child can do

- The case studies are there to help you decide which checklists to use.

- Use the checklists to identify what the child can do. This will guide you towards deciding what the child can be helped to do next.

- You may wish to focus on one checklist or all six. You will already have an idea for some children which area to focus on. For other children, work through the checklists to highlight their needs.

- The checklists are divided into three age groups (5–7 years, 7–9 years and 9–11 years). Use the part of the checklist which matches the child's age.

- Tick the behaviours which the child can do consistently. Children who do not achieve ticks for all the behaviours in the age range will have a difficulty in that area. For these children check the skills in the age group below his age.

- When you have identified the areas in which the child has difficulties, find the corresponding chapter. There you will find general strategies for helping the child learn in class, as well as activities for developing particular skills.

- The checklists can be used at a later date to measure the child's progress over time.

- All six areas in **Thinking and Speaking** overlap. A child may have a difficulty in more than one area. For example, a child who cannot find the right word may also have difficulty speaking in sentences.

# Thinking of Ideas – Case Study

Jodie is 9 years old. She often copies the behaviour of others and gets into trouble because she does not always judge when this is inappropriate. Jodie often takes time to get started on activities particularly if these require her to think in a creative way. In written work Jodie prefers to write about her own experiences rather than use her imagination. Jodie does not yet know how to ask questions to guide her thinking. She tends to ask questions which limit the amount of information gained. For example, asking 'Is it a dog?' before asking 'Is it an animal?'. In group work Jodie tends to echo the ideas of others and usually says 'I don't know' if asked to contribute an idea of her own. Although she can usually suggest a solution to a problem or make a prediction, Jodie can rarely offer an alternative.

# Thinking of Ideas Checklist

Name: _____  Date: _____

Date of Birth: _____

| 5 TO 7 YEARS | TICK |
|---|---|
| Contributes ideas to group discussion. | |
| Uses words related to thinking (e.g. idea, think, realise, imagine, wonder). | |
| Questions others to find out information (e.g. How? What? Where? When? Who?). | |
| Joins in with make-believe activities, acting out his or her own experiences. | |
| **7 TO 9 YEARS** | |
| Thinks of a range of ideas on 'brainstorming' activities. | |
| Talks about his or her own thinking, explaining how one idea has led to another. | |
| Asks questions which show a novel idea or perspective (e.g. Supposing? What if?). | |
| Shows imagination and ideas which extend beyond his or her own experience. | |
| **9 TO 11 YEARS** | |
| Thinks of original ideas and challenges accepted ideas. | |
| Evaluates his or her own thinking, identifying what worked well and what he or she would change next time. | |
| Asks a range of questions to develop his or her own ideas (e.g. Is there another way?). | |
| Makes creative connections between different pieces of information. | |

# Organising Ideas – Case Study

Kieran is 11 years old and in recent years has made considerable progress with listening and understanding. Kieran needs time to express his ideas. Conversation moves too quickly for him and he finds it difficult to get a turn to speak. Kieran only joins in group discussion if directly invited to do so. He does not easily assert his ideas and feelings and is considered to be very passive. In conversation Kieran often starts speaking and then gives up saying 'It doesn't matter'. Although Kieran often has a new perspective to add to the conversation, his words and ideas come out in a jumble. Kieran is socially able with adults and younger children although has been bullied by his age peers in the past.

# Organising Ideas Checklist

| Name: _____ | Date: _____ |
|---|---|
| Date of Birth: _____ | |

| 5 TO 7 YEARS | TICK |
|---|---|
| Retells a familiar story or event in sequence (e.g. and, then). | |
| Focuses on the main point. | |
| Plans what he or she intends to do ahead of doing it (e.g. lists equipment needed for a task). | |
| **7 TO 9 YEARS** | |
| Uses words to signal time and sequence (e.g. before, after a while, meanwhile, during). | |
| Sifts relevant detail from irrelevant information. | |
| Plans a story with a clear beginning, middle and end. | |
| **9 TO 11 YEARS** | |
| Organises information from a range of sources and presents in one simple format (e.g. flow chart, labelled diagram, time line). | |
| Assembles and sequences points in order to support his or her point of view. | |
| Uses different ways of planning (e.g. notes, mind maps, diagrams). | |

# Finding the Right Words – Case Study

Asta is 10 years old and describes herself as being shy and a worrier. When Asta first started school she did not speak to any adults and only sometimes to other children. She remains reluctant to speak to unfamiliar people and rarely joins in class discussion. When Asta is talking she often gets so far and then forgets what she is saying. Asta will sometimes break mid-sentence and take a long pause before continuing. She often uses words inappropriately although they usually have some connection to what she is trying to say. Asta can rarely get her ideas across without a struggle and often relies on her friends to speak for her.

# Finding the Right Words Checklist

| Name: _____ Date: _____ | |
| Date of Birth: _____ | |

| 5 TO 7 YEARS | TICK |
|---|---|
| 'Finds' words quickly and automatically. | |
| Uses a range of verbs types (see examples below). | |
| Selects the right word for the meaning intended (e.g. cabbage/lettuce). | |
| 7 TO 9 YEARS | |
| 'Finds' words quickly and automatically. | |
| Includes detail in descriptive or creative story telling or writing. | |
| Uses words accurately in the right situation. | |
| 9 TO 11 YEARS | |
| 'Finds' words quickly and automatically. | |
| Uses similar sounding words appropriately (e.g. explanation/exclamation). | |
| Expresses ideas with precision. | |

## Some examples of different verb types:

Intransitive verbs require a subject, e.g. I <u>jump</u>.
Transitive verbs require a subject and a direct object, e.g. I <u>kicked</u> the ball.
Ditransitive verbs require a subject, a direct object and an indirect object e.g. I <u>gave</u> Jamie a biscuit.

# Speaking in Sentences – Case Study

Farid is 8 years old. He has experience of three languages and his first language was Baluchi. Baluchi is still spoken by other family members at home although Farid almost always uses English himself. Looking back Farid 's mother says that he showed difficulties with speaking early on and found Baluchi just as difficult as English. Farid is able to hold a simple conversation although frequently becomes frustrated trying to express himself. He often gets words in the wrong order. He uses the present tense even when referring to events in the past or future and confuses pronouns. He uses simple sentences to express his ideas and rarely adds detail. Farid needs 1:1 support from his teacher in order to complete written tasks. He is slow to get written work completed and his sentences are often nonsensical. Farid has an excellent memory for facts and is skilled in some areas of maths. He is popular with his peers and is a keen footballer.

# Speaking in Sentences Checklist

Name: _____ Date: _____
Date of Birth: _____

| 5 TO 7 YEARS | TICK |
|---|---|
| Includes all 'function' words within a sentence (e.g. the, is, does). | |
| Includes all parts of the sentence expected for the verb used (e.g. Ben gave Naomi the car). | |
| Links ideas together using 'and', 'because', 'then'. | |
| Uses words in the right order (e.g. the 'two spotty dogs' not 'the spotty two dogs'). | |
| **7 TO 9 YEARS** | |
| Includes all word endings in a sentence (e.g. circle**s**, add**ed**). | |
| Uses irregular past tenses (e.g. drew, caught). | |
| Uses connectives to express time order, conditional and causal relationships (e.g. before, after, unless, if, so). | |
| Reverses word order to ask questions (e.g. Have you seen my bag?). | |
| **9 TO 11 YEARS** | |
| Uses the same tense throughout a spoken or written narrative. | |
| Uses phrasal verbs appropriately (e.g. carry on, carry out, hold out, hold up). | |
| Uses a wide range of connectives within spoken and written work (e.g. nevertheless, however, furthermore). | |
| Knows the difference between standard and dialectal forms of English. | |

# Speaking Clearly – Case Study

Fabian was a poor and messy eater and dribbled until fairly recently. Fabian also seemed to be permanently congested and still breathes though his mouth. Fabian was early to start talking and has always had a lot to say for himself. However, as a preschooler he confused many speech sounds and went through a phase of stammering. At 5 years old, Fabian's speech sounds slurred and indistinct. He misses out sounds and uses unusual vowel sounds when speaking in sentences. Fabian has many ideas although is sometimes reluctant to speak in class.

# Speaking Clearly Checklist

Name: _____    Date: _____

Date of Birth: _____

| 5 TO 7 YEARS | TICK |
|---|---|
| Speech is understood by most people most of the time. | |
| Uses the sounds 's', 'sh' and 'ch' appropriately when speaking. | |
| Uses double blends at the beginning and ends of words when speaking (e.g. star, pink). | |
| Uses intonation to express meaning (e.g. rising intonation for questions). | |
| **7 TO 9 YEARS** | |
| Produces most words accurately (e.g. 'chicken pox' not 'chicken pops', 'spaghetti' not 'psghetti'). | |
| Uses the sounds 'r' and 'th' (if part of the dialect) appropriately when speaking. | |
| Uses triple blends at the beginning and ends of words when speaking (e.g. straw, bumps). | |
| Keeps rhythm with a poem or song. | |
| **9 TO 11 YEARS** | |
| Speech is easily understood even when he or she is speaking quickly or expressing complicated ideas. | |
| Repeats new multisyllabic words in full, accurately and without effort (e.g. condensation, encyclopaedia). | |
| Stresses certain words in a sentence to change the meaning (e.g. 'Thanks a lot!' said sarcastically). | |

# Thinking and Speaking in Conversation – Case Study

James is 6 years old. He often seems to be in a 'world of his own'. James happily talks about his own experiences at news time although shows little interest in what the other children have to say. He often assumes that people know what he is talking about and can become impatient if people do not understand. James does not always look up when his name is called and when he does join in the conversation his turn does not always fit in with what has gone before. Other children appear intrigued by James. He talks to objects as if they were real and is often unaware of what the rest of the class are doing.

## Thinking and Speaking in Conversation Checklist

| | |
|---|---|
| **Name:** _____ | **Date:** _____ |
| **Date of Birth:** _____ | |

| *5 TO 7 YEARS* | *TICK* |
|---|---|
| Knows what information his or her listener needs to be able to understand. | |
| Takes his or her turn in conversation – sharing ideas and experiences. | |
| Speaks to different people – both children and adults. | |
| *7 TO 9 YEARS* | |
| Knows when his or her listener has misunderstood and clarifies what he or she has said. | |
| Takes his or her turn in conversation – following on from and adding to what other people say. | |
| Speaks confidently to a range of people in a range of situations. | |
| *9 TO 11 YEARS* | |
| Knows how to adjust his or her language to suit the purpose of the activity and his or her audience. | |
| Takes his or her turn in discussion, qualifying or justifying what she or he has said in response to other people's questions and ideas. | |
| Interests others in what she or he has to say (e.g. uses humour, exaggeration, persuasion). | |

# Thinking of Ideas

*'The thinking child is a learning child'.\**
Robert Fisher

*'I would imagine we could put the two slides together and have a big long whizzing slide'*
Sam, Aged 6

## Ideas and thinking styles

Ideas are what the mind creates when it thinks. These ideas are constantly being added to and updated as we take in new information and do more thinking. As we understand more so we can think of new ideas.

Ideas are created by our experiences. We experience the world through our senses, for example sight, hearing, touch, smell and taste. Ideas can be created in many different ways. Sometimes people think in pictures and at other times in words or perhaps in sounds and smells.

As well as creating ideas in different forms, people use ideas to think in different ways. The terms 'inchworm' and 'grasshopper' were originally coined by Bath, Chinn and Knox in Test of Cognitive Style in Mathematics 1986. The 'inchworm' thinks in a linear way moving one step at a time towards the bigger picture. The 'grasshopper' hops from one idea to the next, starting with the bigger picture, and then adding the detail.

---

\*Reproduced with the permission of Nelson Thornes Ltd from *Teaching Children to Learn* – Robert Fisher – ISBN 0 7487 2091 X, first published in 1995

Some children may think of ideas at speed. Others prefer to have more thinking time. To be effective thinkers all children need the time and opportunity to evaluate their thoughts.

# Thinking and speaking

When children speak they are telling us what they are thinking. By speaking about their ideas they are developing them further. Speaking is the link between thinking and writing. Being able to speak about their ideas is a pre-requisite for being able to write about them.

Effective and creative thinking is nurtured when children socialise. Taking part in discussion allows children to share ideas and reflect on their own thinking and develop their problem solving skills.

When young children discuss their ideas they ask one another questions. Asking questions is a vital skill for provoking new thinking and new ideas. Children need to practise asking each other questions before they can ask *themselves* the questions that will develop their own thinking.

# Different kinds of thinking

Children learn to think in different ways for different purposes. **Lower order thinking** involves information and knowledge. For example, working out the steps to make toast.

**Higher order thinking** involves creating new ideas. For example, thinking of a new design for a new toaster.

Consider how a child's thinking changes when asked the following questions.

*Lower order thinking*

1. What colour is a ...?

2. What did the ...?

3. Who ...?

4. What does ... mean?

5. Think of another example of ....

*Higher order thinking*

1. Why do you think ...?

2. What might have happened if ...?

3. How do ...?

4. What are the reasons why ...?

5. Is there another solution to this problem?

Questions are therefore a powerful way to guide a child's thinking and for him to extend and elaborate his ideas.

# The skills needed to think of ideas

Words are the 'windows' to how a child thinks and experiences the world. When a child answers a question in class, his answer will usually give clues to how effectively he is thinking. The child who eloquently answers questions, is showing he can gather his thoughts together and put them across in a way that others will understand. The knowledge that he can get his meaning across with ease builds his self-esteem.

The child who finds it difficult to express himself may be struggling to create fluent thoughts in his head. He may feel frustrated by his ineffective efforts to communicate and may give up because they are met with failure. Successive failure leads him to low self-esteem.

These are some of the skills children need in order to think of ideas:

- Well organised information in their minds, with links to other information they know.
- Good long-term memory so they can retrieve the information they know.
- Good working memory so they can hold ideas in their minds while they decide if it is relevant.
- Knowledge of which thinking style or combination of styles is most appropriate to the situation. For example, logical, creative or reflective thinking.

If a child lacks one or more of the above skills, thinking is made more difficult.

# Help with thinking of ideas

Thinking develops over time and improves with practice and teaching. Strategies can be used to help the child create ideas in different ways. The child needs to know when his thinking style fits the activity and how to ask questions to extend and evaluate his thinking.

## Teacher strategies

Do:

- **Accept a child's idea and value it.**
  Children who feel valued will take risks in their thinking.

- **Avoid talking while children are thinking**.
  Listening and thinking at the same time can be very difficult for some children.

- **Give children a quiet place to think**.
  Noise can interfere with thinking. Some children cannot think in a noisy classroom. Others need quiet background noise to be able to think.

- **Give children time to think.**
  Children need time to process information and form their ideas. Some children need more time to think than others.

- **Listen to the questions that children ask.**
  Their questions can be diverse and add to the repertoire of questions we might ask.

- **Use questions to develop thinking.**
  Use lower and higher order questions to develop different kinds of thinking.

- **Devise activities where children can think of and ask questions.**
  The more children ask questions the more they think.

- **Teach the vocabulary of thinking, for example, 'idea', 'think', 'belief', 'wonder'.**
  Labelling thinking can help a child to understand it.

- **Teach the child to think in pictures.**
  Visualising ideas can be a first step in developing them.

- **Ask the child to draw the visual picture they have in their head.**
  This allows for more thinking about the idea and makes the idea permanent for the child.

- **Ask the child to talk about the picture they have in their head or have drawn.**
  Verbalising ideas helps some children to understand them better.

- **Use puppets, small doll play and drama to act out ideas.**
  Acting out ideas can help a child put his ideas into words.

- **Summarise and recap where the child has reached in his thinking.**
  This can help him move forward in his thinking if he is struggling to think of the right words.

- **Use 'brain storming' and 'mind mapping' activities.**
  This helps the child gather his ideas.

- **Ask children to talk in pairs or very small groups to discuss a problem.**
  This can provide new ways of looking at the problem and helps them to develop their thinking.

# Help with thinking of ideas

## *Child strategies*

- **Have a go at thinking in pictures.**
  This helps you to form your ideas.

- **Draw pictures for your ideas.**
  Seeing your idea in a picture can help you to speak about it.

- **Write any word or sentence you can think of to describe your picture.**
  Seeing your idea in a picture can help you to speak and write about it.

- **Learn to make Mind Maps for your ideas.**
  Mind Maps help you to link ideas and information.

- **Practise asking questions.**
  Asking your own questions makes you think more.

- **Talk to someone else about your ideas. Ask them what they think.**
  Talking about your ideas is one of the best ways to help you think of more ideas.

- Use an Internet search engine, such as 'Google' to look up information on a subject.
  Finding out information can be a first step to thinking of your own ideas.

- Go to the library and ask the librarian to find a book on your topic which has lots of pictures.
  Pictures can help you think of ideas.

- Ask an adult to help you find information for your ideas.
  Working with someone else is a good way of thinking of new ideas.

# *Thinking of Ideas*

## Ask me another!

1. Photocopy the pictures and stick each one on a piece of card.

2. To start with, play the game using one item from *each* category, for example, dog, car, apple, (categories: animals, vehicles, food). Place the cards face down on the table.

3. Take it in turns to take a card. The other player asks questions to guess what is on the card. The adult can model appropriate questions for the child, for example 'Is it a living thing?'

4. Make the game more difficult by including several items within the *same* category, for example, cat, lion. This will require the child to ask different questions and so think in a different way.

5. Add new categories and pictures to make the game more challenging.

## *Thinking of Ideas*

# What could this be?

Choose an object such as a ball.

Pass the ball around the circle.

Each player says what the object could be. For example, an orange, a globe, an apple, a goldfish bowl.

If the player finds it difficult to come up with an idea give a meaning clue. For example, 'What kind of fruit is round and has pips and a core?'

Use other objects in the activity. For example, a pencil, a box, a ruler, a paperweight, a Smarties™ tube.

# *Thinking of Ideas*

## Word brainstorms

This activity provides the child with a visual record of his ideas. The ideas can be used for story telling or in descriptive work.

Think of 4 nouns which go with the adjective salty.

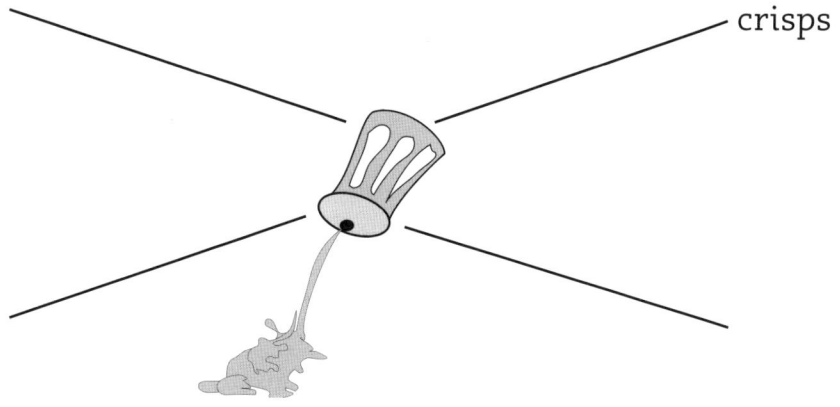

crisps

Think of 6 adjectives to describe a slug.

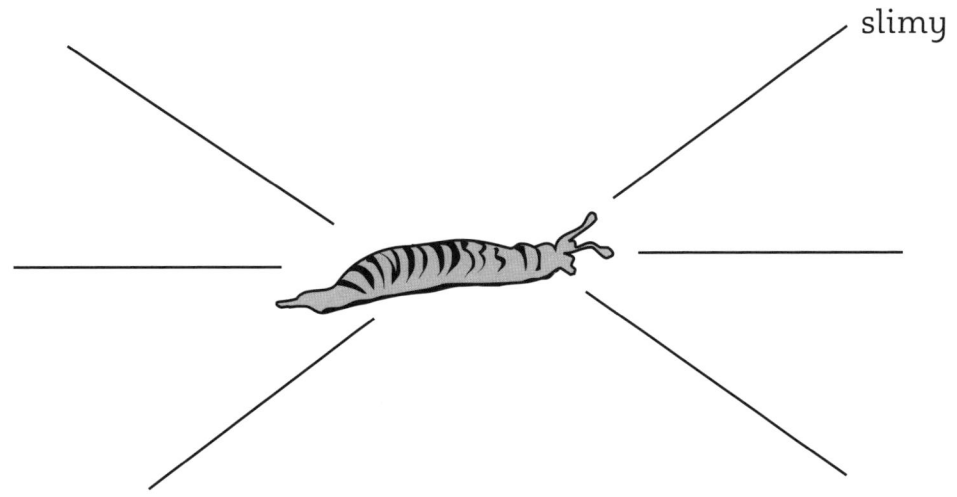

slimy

*Cont'd*

Think of 8 verbs to describe what your body does.

stretch

Think of 3 adverbs that describe the verb run.

quickly

# Puzzle link

Write or draw an idea in the first jigsaw piece. Make it link with the next idea.

Discuss the ideas and how you got to the end from your starting point.

Use this activity to think of and link ideas for a story.

*Start:* ⟶

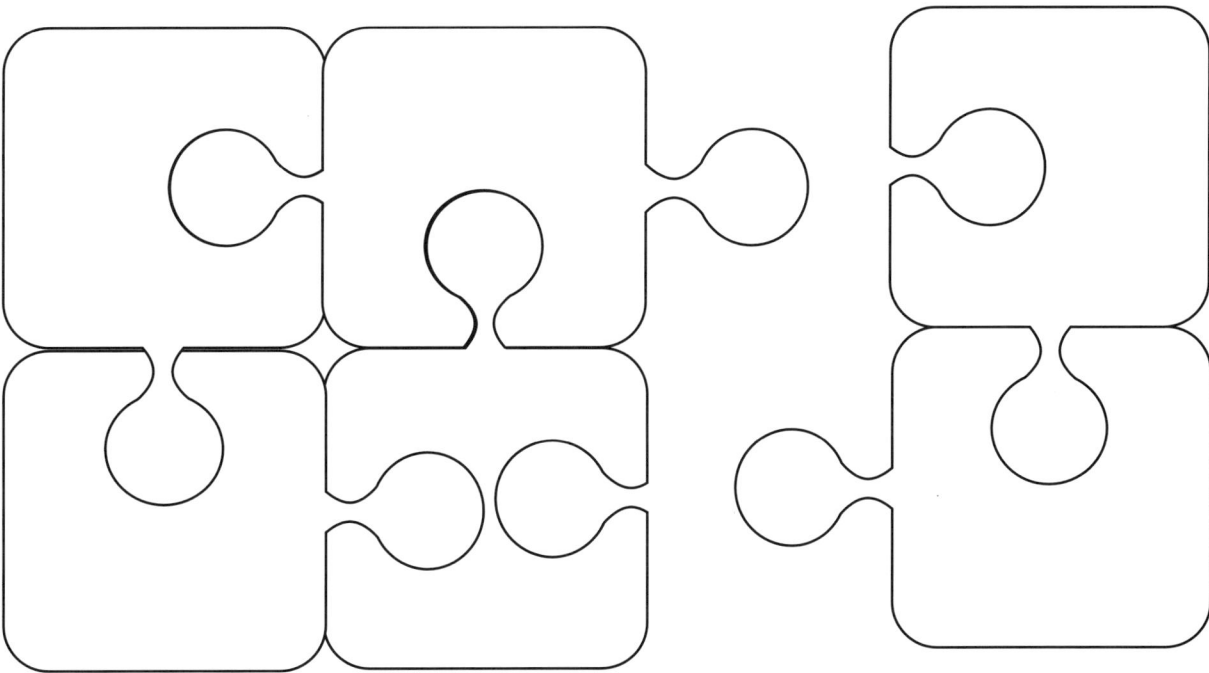

*Finish* ⟵

# Save the planet and make money – a recycling activity!

1. Think of as many original and crazy ideas to use up the left-over items listed below.

2. Talk in twos or in small groups.

3. Make one of your crazy ideas!

The ring pulls from canned drinks could be made into:

- a necklace or a ring

- a musical instrument such as a rattle

- a sculpture or art collage

- a hula hoop for a small insect

- a bubble blower

Other left-over things to recycle:

- peach stones

- empty yogurt pots

- empty kitchen roll holders

- empty plastic water bottles, large or small

## Thinking of Ideas

# Space survival!

1. You are astronauts on your way back to earth from a space mission.
2. You have a problem heating the living sections of the space ship.
3. To keep warm you must all cram into one section of the space ship for the last three days of your journey home.
4. There is limited space for all of you *and* your equipment.
5. Photocopy the Space survival – items + cut up.
6. You can only take 5 of the items on the next page with you for survival.
7. As a group, pick one item from the pack then lay it on the table so everyone can see it. Discuss how it might be useful.
8. Pick the next item. Discuss what use it might be. Decide if it would be more or less useful than the previous item.
9. Place it above or below the other item depending on whether it is more or less important than the previous item.
10. Continue picking items and discussing where they should be placed in relation to those already picked.

The top five items are the ones the group has decided it can't manage without and will take with them.

*Cont'd*

# Space survival! – Items

bottles of water

space suits

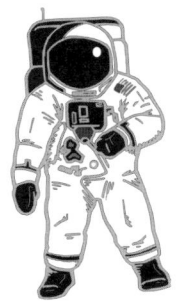

a torch

a bottle of champagne

a digital camera

a game boy

a laptop

spare oxygen tanks

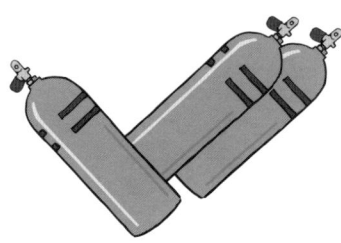

solar panels

map of the earth

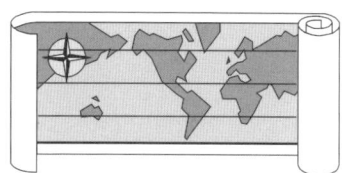

# Speak to someone else about your ideas

# Be a detective

# Look for information

# Think in pictures

# Brainstorm your ideas

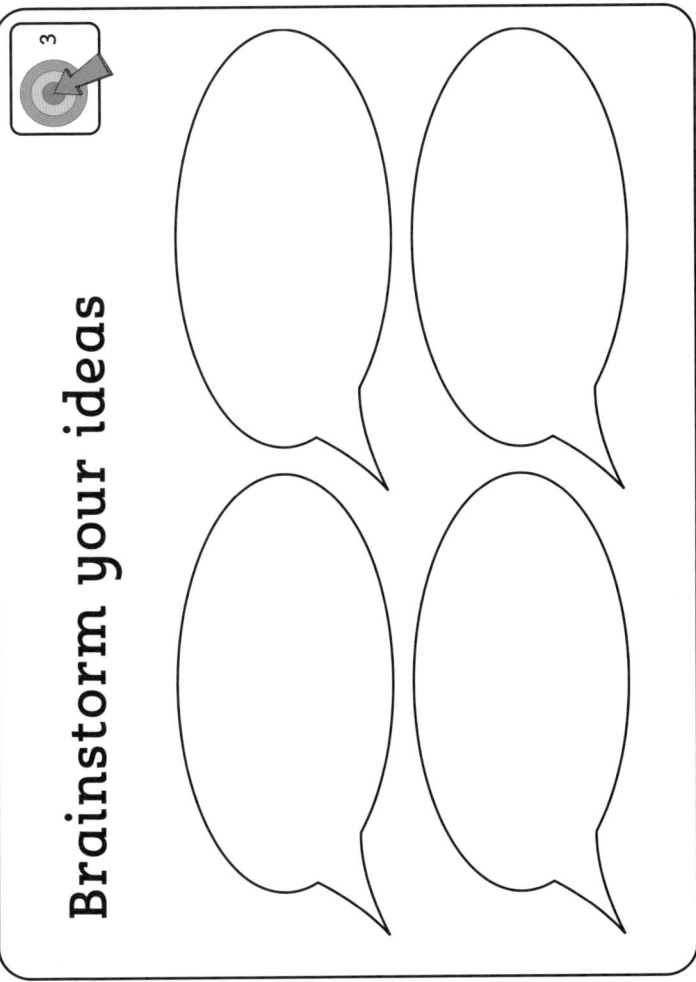

Be whacky and inventive

Make your own target card

Ask thinking questions

Why?          What else?

How?

What reason?

Make your own target card

Target Thinking and Speaking in Primary Schools – 1 Thinking of Ideas

# Organising Ideas

*'Before the teenager has to get first from his behind the next lady her had to wait.'*

Oscar aged 6

## Making sense of the world

Children make sense of their world when information is organised. Once a child has enough information he can start linking it together. The more links a child makes between different pieces of information, the more creative he can be.

When a child takes in new information he re-shuffles what he already knows. So for example, a child learns that mammals breathe air and live on land, while fish breathe through gills and live in the sea. When he learns that dolphins are mammals and live in the sea, he may re-shuffle his original thinking in order to understand the new information.

The process of re-shuffling information is happening all the time in a child who is an effective learner.

## Different ways of organising

We need to be able to organise information in different ways to support different kinds of thinking. When children organise their ideas they are sifting information and deciding if it is relevant or irrelevant to the topic. Effective organisers can rapidly access relevant information and ideas for their thinking.

When ideas are organised serially it helps children to think in a logical way. An 'inchworm' thinks in this way. This is important for planning and thinking ahead, for example changing for PE, writing a list, and putting forward an argument.

Organising information in a flexible way enables us to be creative. A 'grasshopper' is good at thinking in this way. This can be helpful for solving problems such as how to choose the best players for a football team. It can also help us link information in new ways, e.g. Mind Maps.

Children who find it hard to think in words may prefer to act out their ideas. Children who learn by 'doing' might like to create a 3D model in clay.

It is important that children are given the opportunity to learn a variety of different ways to organise their ideas. This will give them the opportunity to think in different ways too.

# Memory and organising information

There can be a heavy load placed on **long-term**, **short-term** and **working memory** when a child is asked to organise his thoughts and gather information for a purpose. For example, if asked to imagine himself as Isambard Brunel, a child will use short-term memory to remember what he has been asked to do. He will then recall and gather information from long-term memory. After that he will use working memory to hold the information and ideas while he sifts and sorts to work out which ones are relevant.

It is important to make the information and ideas easy for the child to remember and manipulate. This could be in a visual form for the child who thinks in pictures. It could be achieved by recording the child's thoughts on a tape recorder if he thinks in spoken words or sound.

# Planning for writing

Strategies which help children to write can also be used to support children in their thinking and speaking. For example, a 'writing frame' is a good way of organising a child's ideas for speaking as well as writing. It can include gathering appropriate vocabulary and working out the logical sequence of events or arguments.

'Scaffolding' also provides an opportunity to talk about ideas and plan with the teacher. The teacher links new information to what the child already knows. Experimenting with ideas and evaluating them is part of scaffolding. Experimenting and evaluating in speaking is as important as experimenting and evaluating in writing.

Children who are taught how to structure and organise their ideas can become better thinkers as a consequence.

# Talking about organising

An effective organiser of ideas will be able to say **how** he organised his ideas. He will be able to concentrate on the task until it is complete. His success will give him positive feedback and help his self-esteem.

A child who cannot organise his ideas will not be able to say how he might go about the task. He will find it hard to concentrate because he will not know what to focus on. He may also find the task overwhelming. His failure to organise information will damage his self-esteem and he may behave in a disruptive way or produce little work.

A child who is unable to organise his idea will benefit from talking with an adult who can **show him ways** to organise his ideas. These ways will need to be concrete such as tape recording ideas or drawing them. Bridging the gap between thinking and writing must include speaking.

# The skills needed to organise ideas

To be effective organisers, children need to:

- talk about their planning and organising, with other children and adults
- understand the goal so a plan can be made
- decide what information is appropriate and relevant to the activity
- use memory to recall information and ideas
- understand the 'main idea' and the 'detail' relating to a task
- organise information in different ways, for example, lists, writing frames, Mind Maps
- use words of time and sequence, for example 'first, next, and then'
- concentrate for the period of planning
- monitor the success of how the information is organised
- check that the way they have organised the information fits the situation

A child who can't organise his ideas will not be able to draw on his knowledge to think ideas through. He will find it more difficult to learn and remember new information.

# Help with organising ideas

*Teacher strategies*

Do:

- **Be positive about a child's efforts.**
  He may be trying out ideas. Give him credit for 'having a go'.

- **When presenting information in class, start with an overview, then talk about the details.**
  This will show the child one way of organising information.

- **Teach the child different ways of organising his ideas according to the task.**
  This helps the child learn how to use different organisation strategies flexibly.

- **Teach the child how to plan with a beginning, middle and end.**
  This will provide a framework for information that has to be presented in serial order.

- **Use prompt words or phrases such as 'first, then, after' to organise what he wants to say.**
  This can help the child who cannot work out for himself what the next step is and model how to use these words.

- **Break tasks into very small steps to provide a structure. For example, provide the beginning of the story for the child to finish. Tell a story in the round.**
  This provides a model for the child and allows him to focus on one manageable part of the task.

- **Use Post-Its™ for writing down and organising information.**
  The ideas can be moved around easily.

- **Check and give feedback frequently.**
  When children are trying out a new or difficult skill they need reassurance that the way they are approaching the task is appropriate.

- **Allow children to work together to organise and plan.**
  This can help those children who are not ready to work independently.

- **Sometimes pair children who think in the same way to work together.**
  Organising ideas together can be helpful if both children think the same way.

- **Sometimes pair children who think in very different ways to work together.**
  Discussing different ways of organising information can lead to more creative thinking.

- **Ask the child how *he* prefers to organise his ideas.**
  Use whatever the child finds works for him.

- **Talk through with the child how he is organising his ideas.**
  Listening to his own voice helps the child develop inner language which supports memory, planning and thinking.

- **Support a child's ideas with a visual prompt such as written words or a picture.**
  This will provide a record of his ideas.

- **Use a tape recorder or the recording facility on a computer as a verbal scratch pad to record information.**
  This can help those children who benefit from listening again to the information they want to organise.

- **Pre-warn a child that he will be asked to contribute in a lesson.**
  This will give him time to plan what to say.

- Practise with the child what he wants to tell in class, write it down too if he can read well enough.
  This will make him less anxious and help him to remember the activity later.

# Help with organising ideas

## *Child strategies*

- Be prepared to have a go with a new way of organising your work.
  This will give you more options for your learning.

- Gather information first then organise it.
  This will save time and energy.

- Ask for help to get started if you are stuck.
  This can get you 'back on track' and keep you going.

- Brainstorm your ideas, putting them down on paper before you forget.
  You can organise the ideas once you have written them.

- Work with a friend.
  Talking together about your work is an excellent way of learning.

- Work with a scribe, who can jot down ideas for you.
  Then you can organise the ideas, into piles, lists or make links between the ideas.

- If you think in pictures learn how to make a Mind Map.
  This is a visual way of organising information.

- If you think in words, record your ideas onto tape or the computer.
  You can then replay your ideas while you think of how to organise them.

## Telling News

1 Ask parents to fill in the grid below, relating to a recent event the child has taken part in, such as a cinema trip or a walk.

2 Ask the child to bring in something related to the event, such as the cinema ticket, or something found on the walk.

3 Use the grid as a 'prompt' for the child when he's talking so his thoughts are organised.

4 Use the grid to keep the child talking about relevant information.

| |
|---|
| Who was there?  |
| What happened?  |
| Where was it?  |
| When did it happen?  |
| How did you feel?  |
| Why did you feel that way?  |

## What's Next? (Track Game)

1. For each of the activities talk about what the child will need (equipment) and the three steps to do the activity. Then talk about what you might do next.

   'What *equipment* will you need?'
   'What is the **first** step?'
   'What is the **next** step?'
   'What is the **last** step?'

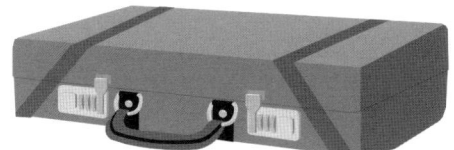

2. Throw the dice and move along the board.

3. Pick up a card each time you land on a square.

4. Each square tells you what you have to talk about.

5. The first person to the finish is the winner.

For those children who have difficulty talking accurately about the steps, ask the child to draw pictures to show the equipment and the order of steps.

For example:

**Making a sandwich**

**Equipment:** 2 slices of bread, butter, filling, knife, plate

**1st step**    Spread the butter with the knife on one side of each slice of the bread.

**2nd step**    Put the filling on one slice of bread.

**3rd step**    Place the other slice butter side down on top of the filling.

**Next step**    Eat it!

*Cont'd*

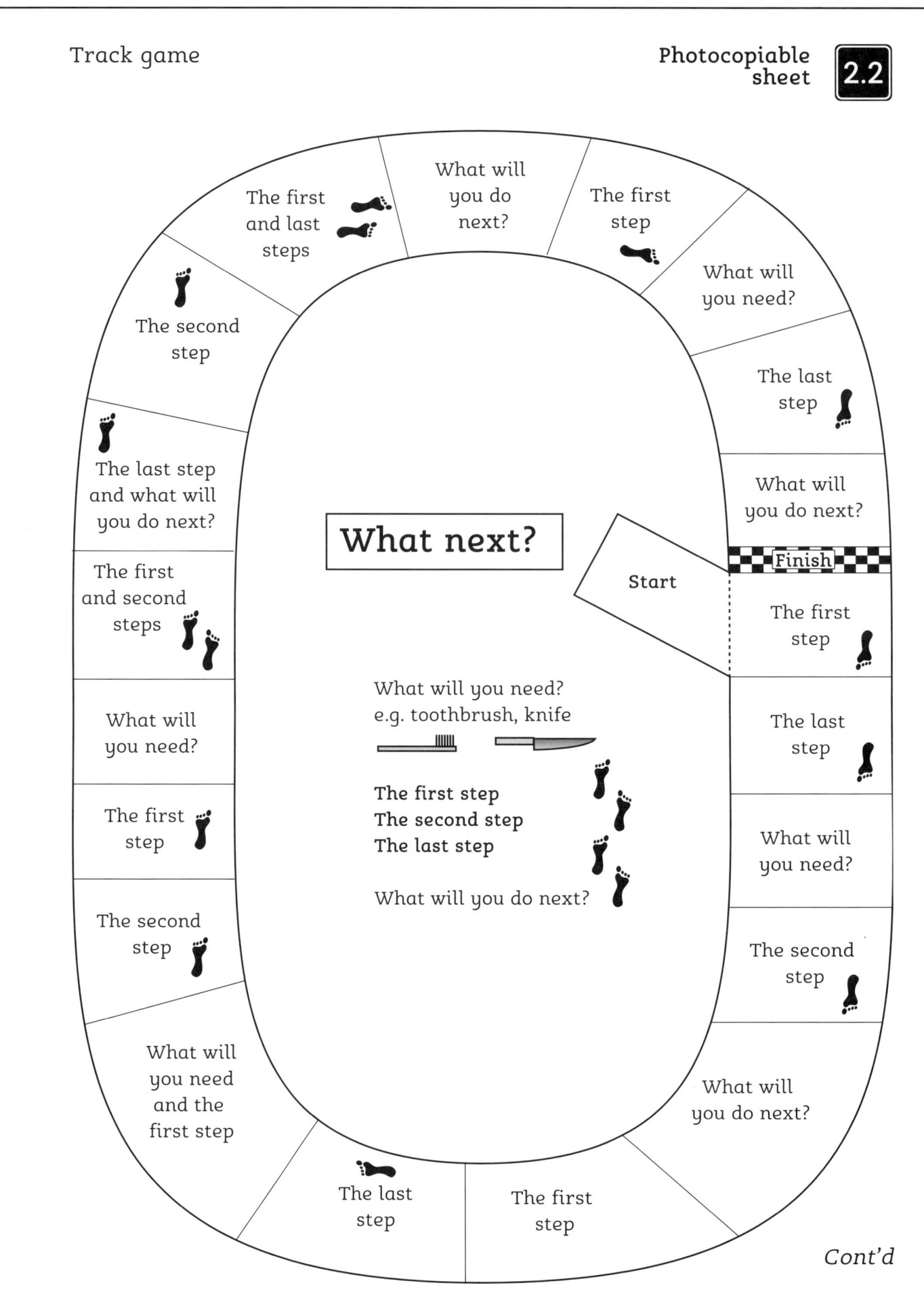

What next?

What will you need?
e.g. toothbrush, knife

The first step
The second step
The last step

What will you do next?

Target Thinking and Speaking in Primary Schools – 2 Organising Ideas

# Cards for Track Game – add your own ideas in the blank spaces

| Cleaning your teeth | Running a bath | Getting dressed |
|---|---|---|
| Going to the park | Going swimming | Pouring a drink |
| Making a sandwich | | |
| | | |

# Talking Tales

1. Photocopy the connectives. Glue them onto blank cards.

2. Choose a story starter from the examples.

3. Take it in turns to continue the story using the connectives.

4. Make sure the last person to pick up a card finishes the story.

## Talking tales: connectives

| at first | then | a bit later |

| until | after | next | later on |

| meanwhile | after a while | soon |

| from then on | eventually | finally |

*Cont'd*

Target Thinking and Speaking in Primary Schools – 2 Organising Ideas

# Talking tales: story starters

Robbie had £50 in
his piggy bank.......

Suddenly all the lights
went out in the house....

The dolphin turned
and swam towards us.

You meet a magic genie.....

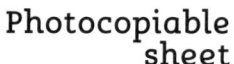 

## Circle of Relevance

[1] Use the circle of relevance with a child or group.

[2] Sift information which is **relevant** or **not relevant** to the topic.

[3] Discuss the reasons for the choice.

[4] Stick the statement in the appropriate circle.

[5] An example is given. Use topics relevant to the child.

## Making a sandwich

- It's Tuesday today.      **Not relevant**

- Spread butter on a slice of bread.      **Relevant**

- You can buy white and brown bread from the supermarket.      **Not relevant**

- Put a slice of cheese on the butter.      **Relevant**

- Tomatoes are round.      **Not relevant**

- Slice tomatoes thinly and put on top of the cheese.      **Relevant**

- Put the top slice of bread on top of the tomato.      **Relevant**

- Cheese can be smelly.      **Not relevant**

*Cont'd*

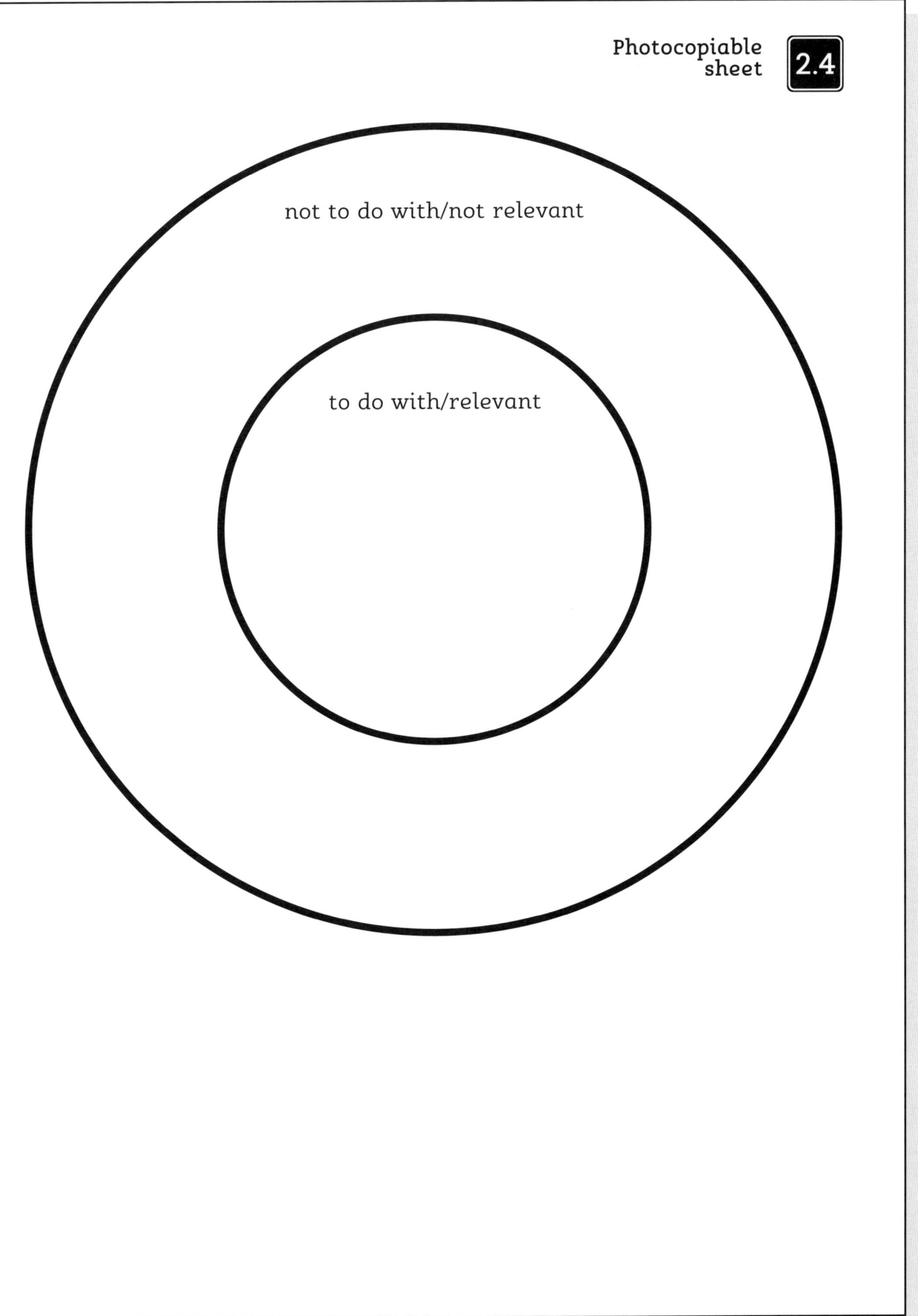

not to do with/not relevant

to do with/relevant

## Speaking Frame for an Argument

# Eating a school lunch is a good idea – discuss!

1  To start with, use the idea provided about eating a school lunch. Later use other ideas as the basis for an argument.

2  Use the 'speaking frame' to record the arguments.

3  The activity can be used in a small group of two or three children. This allows for different ideas and the opportunity for each child to participate. Initially one 'speaking frame' could be used for the whole group. Later each child could have a 'speaking frame' of their own.

4  Ask the children to talk about their ideas 'for' or 'against' having school lunches.

5  Ask the children to write or draw pictures to record the arguments.

6  When all the ideas are recorded, discuss which ones are most important in the 'for' and 'against' columns. Which ones are the least important?

7  Ask different children to talk about **either** the 'for' **or** the 'against' arguments to the rest of the group.

8  Have a vote!

The speaking frame can be used as the basis for writing about an argument once it has been discussed.

*Cont'd*

# Speaking frame for an argument

For example:

| For: | Against: |
|---|---|
| Eating food at midday gives you energy to concentrate and learn in the afternoon. | School lunches contain unhealthy amounts of fat and carbohydrates. |
| There is always a salad at lunch. | There aren't enough healthy choices at lunch. |
| There are plenty of chips. | There are too many chips. |
|  |  |
|  |  |

*Cont'd*

# Speaking frame for an argument – extension activity

The extension activity can be used for one child to summarise all the arguments and give his opinion. Alternatively different children can take different parts of the grid and present the arguments in the round.

| |
|---|
| **There are many different ideas about:**<br><br>**whether eating school lunches are a good idea or not.** |
| Some people think that it's a good idea<br><br>because they think:<br><br>_____<br><br>_____ |
| From a different point of view, other people think that:<br><br>_____<br><br>_____ |
| My own opinion is that _____<br><br>because _____ |

1  Read the passage and highlight relevant information.

2  Label the diagram using the words in the box and referring back to the passage.

3  Find another piece of writing with a diagram of something that interests the child.

4  Copy the diagram and ask the child to label it.

The first Space Shuttle lifted off on 12th April 1981. Two of its purposes are to carry out experiments in space and to transport astronauts to the space station. The Space Shuttle has four main parts. The orbiter, is the main part of the shuttle and it is this part that goes round the earth. At the end of the mission it comes back to earth and lands.

There is one very large fuel tank attached to the middle of the orbiter. There are also two booster rockets at the side of the fuel tank that ensure that it takes off. Heat and flames come out of these boosters. The fuel tank and the two rockets are thrown away after take off. The Space Shuttle programme still continues today after over a hundred flights.

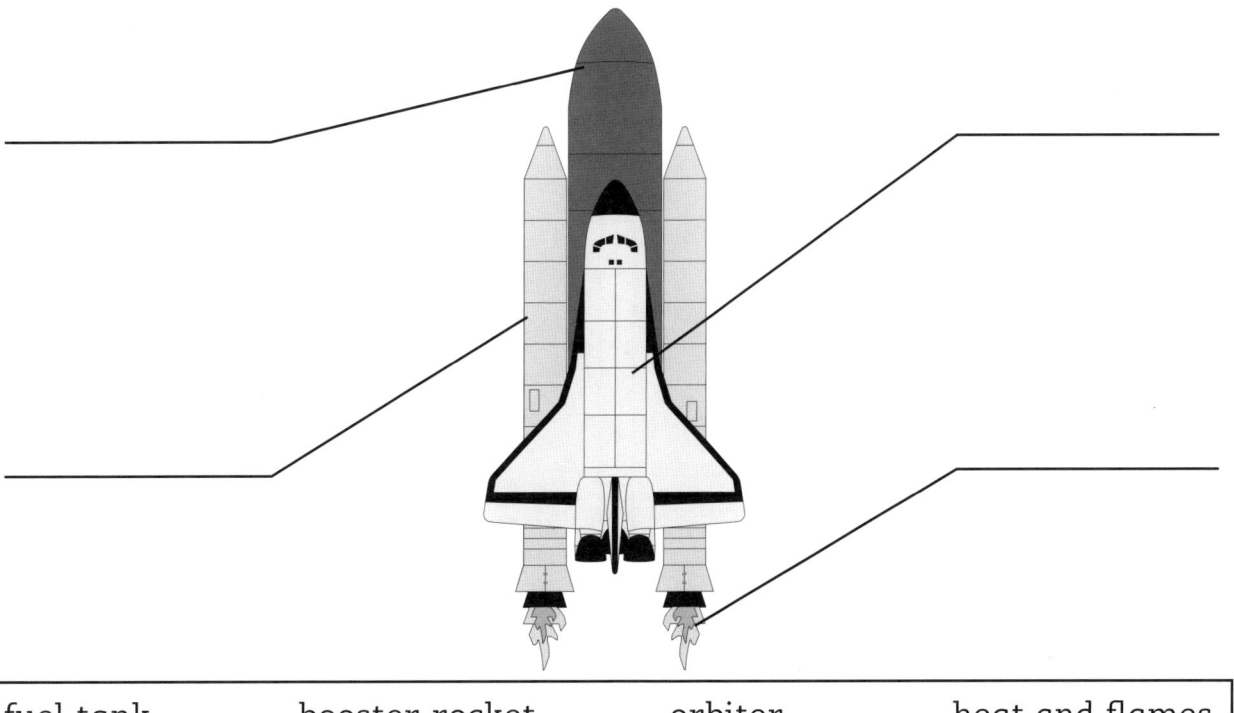

| fuel tank | booster rocket | orbiter | heat and flames |

## Organising ideas

**Plan ahead.**
Equipment

1st step  2nd step  3rd step

## Organising ideas

not
to do with/

to do
with/
relevant

not relevant

## Organising ideas

**Who was
there?**

**What
happened?**

**Where was it?  When was it?**

**How did you
feel?**

**Why did you
feel that way?**

## Organising ideas

Use words to join ideas.

before          after

next            a bit later

in a minute/    after an hour
in a moment

soon            after a while

Target Thinking and Speaking in Primary Schools – 2 Organising Ideas

## Organising ideas

Use diagrams to organise ideas

## Organising ideas

Make your own target card

## Organising ideas

For

Against

## Organising ideas

Make your own target card

# *Finding the Right Words*

**3**

'I know what the word is ... word please come back'
Maya, aged 10

'Delectable, is that the same as delicious?'
Joe, aged 7

## Communicating with words

Words and their meaning are central to the ability to think and are the bridge between thought and communication. When we are precise in our thinking, and can use the right words for these thoughts we can be effective communicators. When we are unable to match precise words to our thinking we will not be able to convey our meaning to others.

Speaking using the right words will also allow us to write with precision. Any difficulty a child experiences using words when talking will be reflected in his writing.

## How words are stored

We create 'representations' of words in our mind. 'Representation' means all the things we know about the word. This will include the meaning of the word, how the word sounds, how we visualise it, as well as how we write it and how the word fits into a sentence. It can also include our feelings when we first heard the word and the context in which we heard it. Effective thinkers create many different representations for a word.

The meaning of the word cat consists of a network of information the child builds up about it.

furry animal                                                    whiskers

meow                                                                tail

He also creates links *between* words with similar meaning, learning how they are similar and how they differ, for example: cat and dog; both are pets but one barks and one meows.

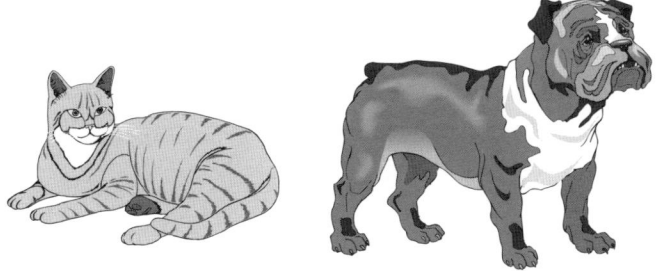

The link will also be made with other animals that are in the cat category, **cat**, **lion**, **cheetah**, **tiger**.

Linking the sound of the word with its meaning /k-a-t/, is dependent upon phonological awareness and making the speech movements for a particular word.

Knowing how the sound of the word is similar to and differs from other words is also important, for example, /cat/cap/, cat/catapult.

The grammatical class a word belongs to enriches the representations of the word. For example 'cat' is a noun and will be used as a subject or an object to a verb in a sentence. For example, 'The black cat chased the white cat.'

The more links we make, the richer the network becomes. This allows us to be more creative in our thinking.

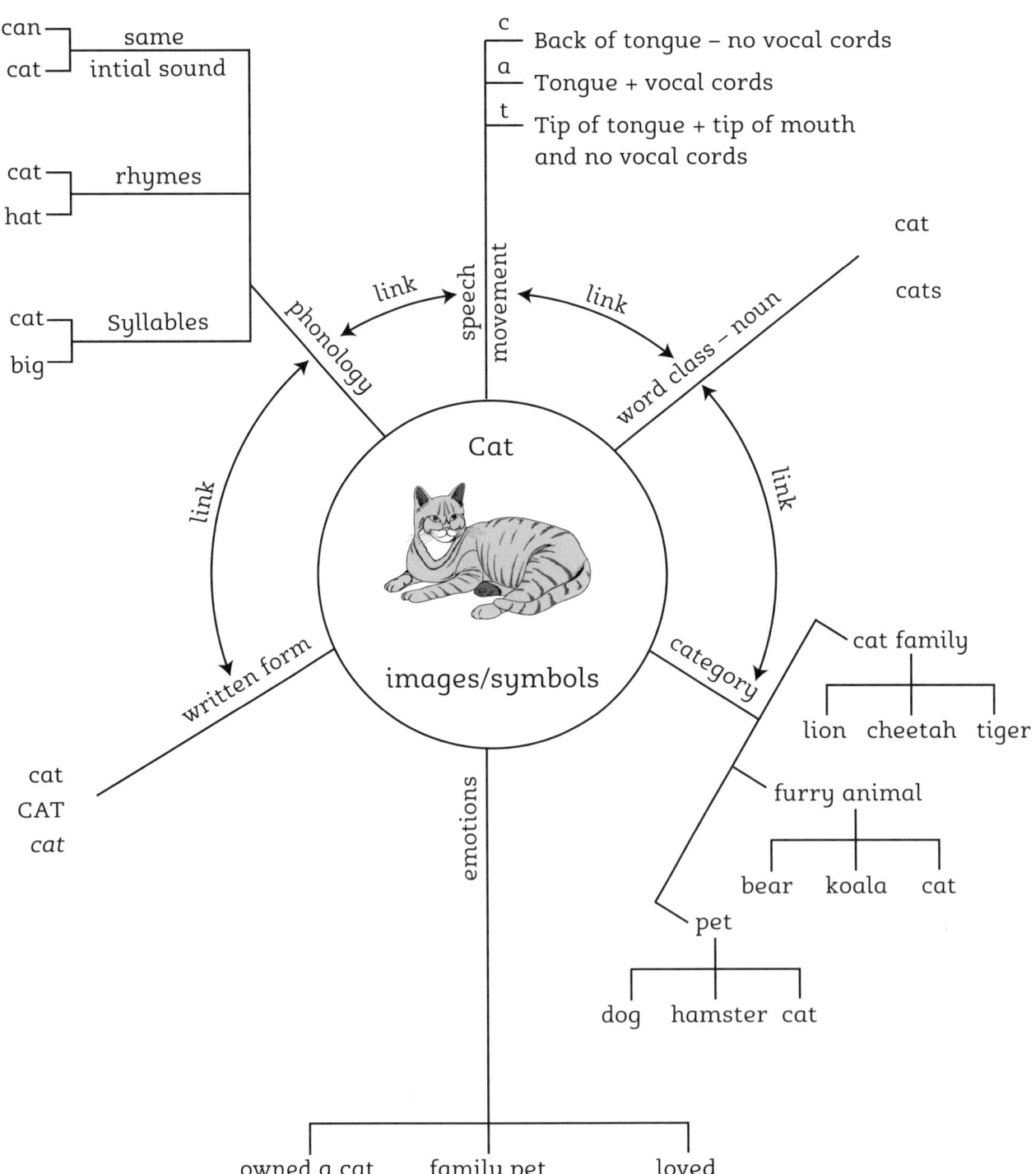

The knowledge we have of a word is not static and changes over time. When we hear the word in a new context, we add information to what we already know about that word.

# Word retrieval

Effective and creative thinkers make many different links between words, creating a highly organised system which makes for easy access to the right word when we speak.

When a child uses a word, he links the **meaning** of the word onto its **sound**. Fast automatic word retrieval depends on this link.

The more times we hear and use a word in context the more automatic its retrieval will be.

In time the child learns, not only what the word sounds like but also what it looks like when it is written. This adds another link to the word so a three-way link exists between its meaning, its sound and its written form.

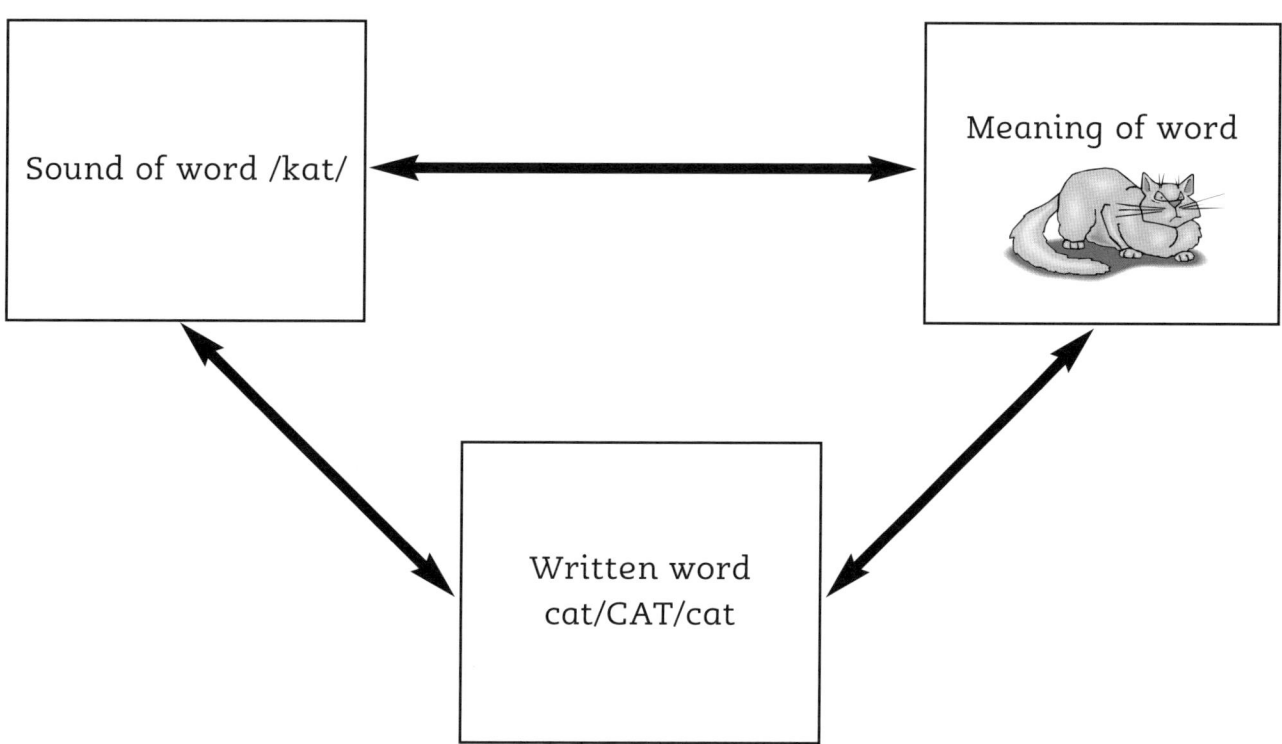

# The skills a child needs to find of the right word

- an understanding of the word's meaning
- the opportunity to hear and practise saying the word
- a link between the word meaning and the sound of the word
- ability to have different representations of the word e.g. sound, picture
- ability to organise words according to their sounds – e.g. words that rhyme with it or start with the same sound
- ability to organise words according to their meaning, same category, opposite, etc.

# What might happen when a child can't retrieve the right word

A child's behaviour can indicate he is experiencing difficulty finding the right words. He may:

- search for the word trying unsuccessfully to be precise
- make frequent pauses as he speaks
- substitute another similar sounding word
- substitute another similar meaning word
- say very little and avoid joining in group discussions
- avoid eye contact
- show his frustration by being angry or withdrawn
- produce written work which contains limited vocabulary
- avoid written work

Children who have difficulty finding the right word for speaking will have difficulty finding the right word when writing. They may also find it hard to engage in fast moving conversation with their peers.

When considering how best to help children who have difficulty finding the right word, consider where the difficulty might lie:

# input > storage > retrieval

**Input** relates to how accurately the word is learnt.

**Storage** is how the word is organised with other words in our memory.

**Retrieval** relates to how the word is recalled when we want to speak.

# Help with finding the right words

Strategies that facilitate how to organise words and make links will support word retrieval when speaking.

*Teacher strategies*

**Do:**

- **Explain the meaning of new words. Talk about it, visualise it, draw it, act it out.**
  Accurate knowledge of word meaning is important for its retrieval.

- **Teach the sound of new vocabulary. For example the number of syllables it has, other words that start with the same sound.**
  Learning the phonology of word aids memory and recall.

- **Teach the child about different types of words such as nouns, verbs, adjectives, adverbs.**
  This adds another link to the word's representation.

- **Give the child a word and ask him to put it into different sentences.**
  Practising the word makes its recall more automatic.

- **Learn a new word in small steps. For example, saying the word, saying the word in a phrase, a sentence, a picture description, a story, everyday conversation.**
  Words occur in different situations and need to be practised in these different places.

- **Give the child time to respond and think of the right word.**
  Effective thinking may take time.

- **Maintain eye contact and show your interest when a child is struggling to think of a word.**
  This ensures the child knows you are listening and that you value what he or she has to say.

- **Cue the word with its first sound or number of syllables.**
  This taps into how the word sounds, its 'phonology'.

- **Teach the child to visualise what he wants to say.**
  Visualising an idea can be a first step towards putting it into words.

- **Ask specific questions to encourage further information.**
  This focuses the child on finding specific words.

- **Offer words for a child's thoughts if he is struggling to put his ideas into words. For example, 'are you imagining something you can eat?'**
  This can help to narrow down the choice of words to choose from.

- Talk to the child about what works for them when they are thinking of words, e.g., visualising, drawing.

  This is meta-cognition which allows a child to understand his best strategies.

- **Find out what kinds of words the child has problems remembering, for example, verbs, new topic words.**

  This enables us to give specific and individualised help to the child.

- **Find ways to cue the child into the word.**

  For example, the first sound or the number of beats.

- **Review and revise new words often.**

  Review and revision is vital for input, storage and retrieval of words.

# Help with finding the right words

## Child strategies

- **Ask for help.**

  It's OK to ask for help so you can keep going with your work.

- **Give yourself time to think.**

  We remember best when we are relaxed.

- **Picture the word in your head, or draw it.**

  Starting with a picture can lead to finding the word.

- **Find a picture of the word.**

  This might help you name the word, or allow someone else to tell you the name.

- **Explain the meaning you want to get across in another way.**

  Talking about the meaning may help you recall the word.

- **Talk about the sound of the word, e.g. the number of syllables, the first sound.**
  The link with sounds can help in remembering a word.

- **If you know a strategy that works for you, use it.**
  This will allow you to be more independent in your learning.

# Comparing and Contrasting Words

What's the same?

What's different?

Version 1 – words with SIMILAR MEANING

1. Choose from the pairs of words below.

2. Explain how the words have similar meaning.

   ● These things are *similar*...
   ● One thing the *same* is...
   ● A *similarity* between these two things is...

3. Explain how the words are *different*.

   ● These words are *different* because...

   ● One thing that *differs* is...

   ● A *difference* between them is...

| | |
|---|---|
| gravel/stones | stool/chair |
| orange/amber | tanker/truck |
| duvet/sleeping bag | scooter/bike |
| band/orchestra | trainers/shoes |
| cheetah/lion | yoghurt/ice cream |
| garage/carport | caravan/tent |

*Cont'd*

Version 2 – SIMILAR SOUNDING words

● These words *sound similar* in this way...
● These words *sound different* because...

purple/turtle                         interior/inferior

slurping/spurting            obstacle/obstinate

spout/sprout                              sliver/silver

tangerine/tambourine        fringe/fridge

or/all            ways/waves            switch/stitch

giraffe/draft            envelope/antelope

core/cork        snout/spout        cuff/calf

explanation/exclamation            seats/sheets

great/grape            resolution/revolution

cartoon/carton            allegation/allocation

Target Thinking and Speaking in Primary Schools – 3 Finding the Right Words

# Word Retrieval Games

You will need a dice, a spinner with numbers 1–3 and an alphabet spinner available from Taskmaster.

Choose a version of the game listed below:

1  category only

2  category + number of syllables

3  category + initial sound

4  category + rhyme

5  category + final sound

# Version 1 – category only
Materials: a dice

1  Pick the category and roll the dice.

2  Name as many members of the category, as the number on the dice.

## Categories

- things to sit on

- things you wear to keep warm

- things you can read

- mammals with fur

- girl's names

- colours

- titles of jobs people do

- different kinds of bread

*Cont'd*

# Version 2 – category + syllable number

Materials: number spinner 1–3

1  Pick a category.

2  Spin the number spinner.

3  Think of words that are in the category and have the same number of syllables as the spinner.

## Categories

- something to sit on: 1 – chair, 2 – sofa, 3 – rocking chair
- things you wear: 1 – fleece, 2 – jumper, 3 – underwear.
- things you write with
- pets
- vehicles
- countries
- names of towns
- things you see in the sky

# Version 3 – category + initial sound

Materials: alphabet spinner

1  Pick a category.

2  Spin the alphabet spinner.

3  Name a word that belongs to the category and starts with that sound. For example, fruit with a /p/ – plum, pineapple, pear, peach.

## Categories:

- vegetables
- clothes
- colours
- means of transport
- boys' names

*Cont'd*

**Target Thinking and Speaking in Primary Schools** – 3 Finding the Right Words

# Version 4 – category + rhyme

1. Play this as a quiz.

2. Ask children in the group, in turn to supply the answer.

## Categories

- an insect that rhymes with tree. (bee)

- a sea mammal that rhymes with tail. (whale)

- a drink that rhymes with toffee. (coffee)

- a vehicle that rhymes with luck. (truck)

- a farm animal that rhymes with boat. (goat)

- a bird that rhymes with carrot. (parrot)

- a shape that rhymes with care. (square)

- a number that rhymes with dirty. (thirty)

# Version 5 – category + final sound

1. Pick a category and spin the alphabet spinner.

2. Name a word which belongs to the category and ends with that sound.

3. This is a real challenge and gets even the adult thinking!

## Categories:

- birds

- people's first names

- pets

- drinks

## Action Stations!

1. This activity makes the child think of the different verbs for the sentence.

2. Read the sentence to the child.

3. Ask him to think of at least two different verbs to fit the sentence.

4. If the child has difficulty working out what verbs would go in the sentence, describe a situation to help them. For example, what might you say if your pen was missing? (taken/stolen)

- The man ................... the door. (painted/closed)

- They ............ their day out. (talked about/planned)

- The lady ................ the pancake. (tossed/ate)

- The boy ............. the ice cream. (sold/licked)

- Cats ........... mice. (chase/like)

- Quick! ......................... the fire. (put out/mind)

- ......................... the wardrobe! (move/shut)

- Have you ............................ my pen. (seen/borrowed)

- I can't ........................the box. (lift/open)

- ........................... the book. (read/give back)

# Descriptive Speaking and Writing

1. Talk about the pictures on the next page. Talk about a situation in which the child has seen or used the items.

2. Get the child to use his senses to think of adjectives connected to the picture (look, sound, touch, taste, smell).

3. Tell the child to 'picture', 'see' or 'visualise' the item move or being used. What action words go with the child's picture? (verbs)

4. Describe *how* the item moves or is used. (adverbs)

5. Write the words the child thinks of on the **word web**. A word web shows how words are connected to one another.

6. Ask the child to use the descriptive words in sentences, e.g. 'A black furry spider scuttled sneakily across the carpet.'

7. Use the sentence for descriptive writing if appropriate.

*Cont'd*

*Verbs*

What does it do?

*Adjectives*

What does it
look/feel/sound like?

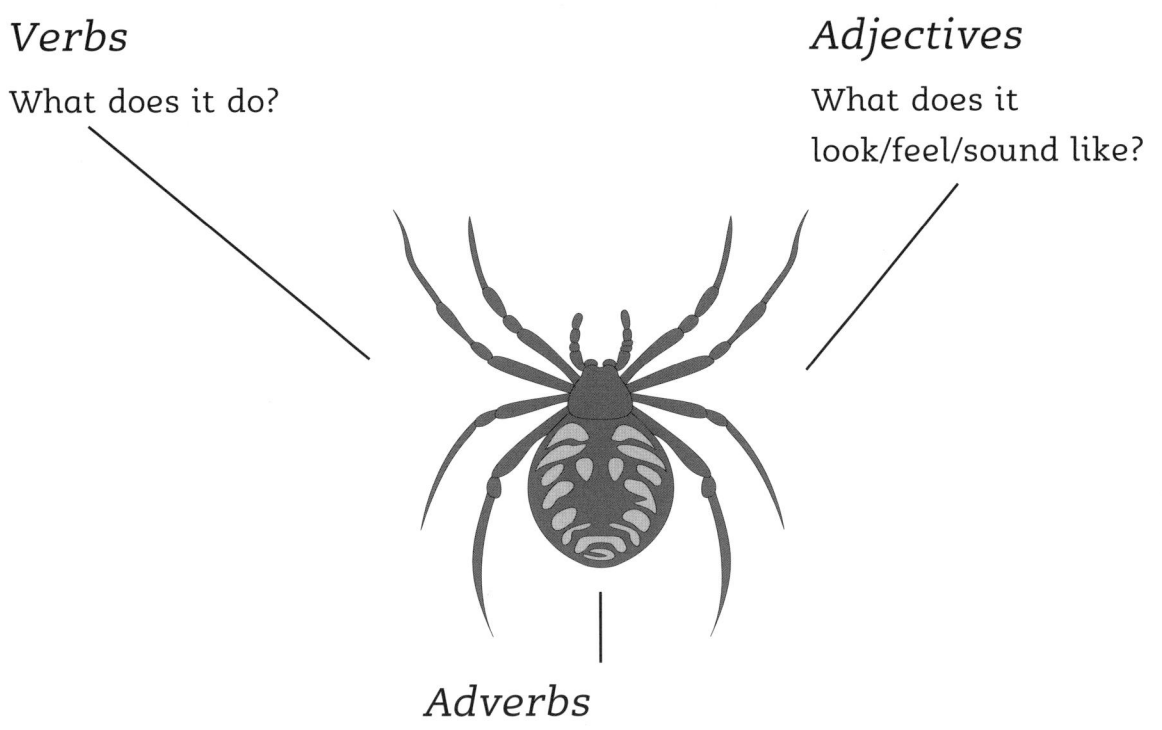

*Adverbs*

How does it move?

*Verbs*

What is it used for?

*Adjectives*

What does it
look/feel/sound like?

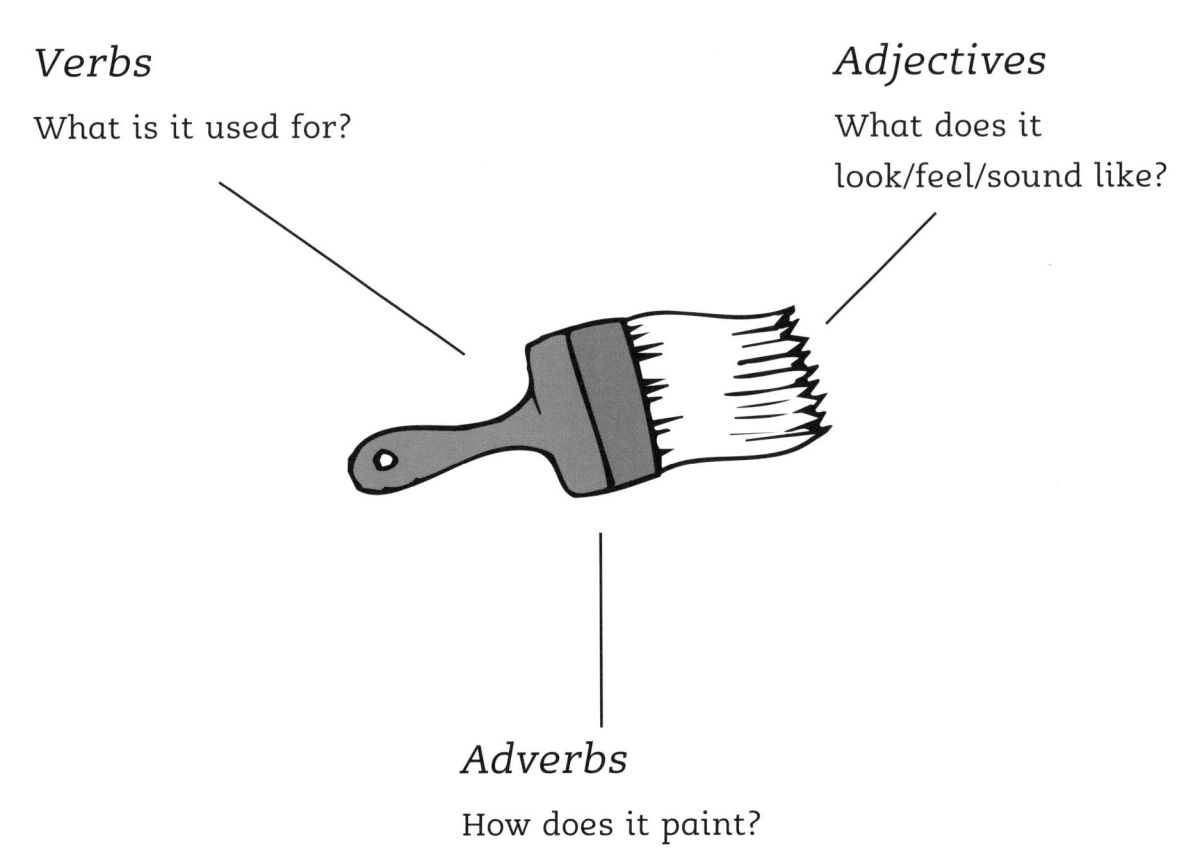

*Adverbs*

How does it paint?

# Anagrams and Semantic Clues

Unscramble the mixed-up letters and use the clue to think of the answer.

| 1 | A fierce king of the jungle. | **nilo** |
| 2 | Another word for thin. | **mils** |
| 3 | A plan for finding your way. | **pam** |
| 4 | A long thin poisonous animal. | **kanes** |
| 5 | A fierce brown furry animal. | **rabe** |
| 6 | A colour. | **lube** |
| 7 | A hot drink. | **eat** |
| 8 | For drinking out of. | **gum** |
| 9 | A small device for giving light. | **plam** |
| 10 | A shape in the night sky. | **rats** |

# Finding the right word 2

Point to the sound at the beginning of the word

abcdefghijklmnopqrstuvwxyz

# Finding the right word 4

Explain what you know about the word

# Finding the right word 1

Make a picture of the word in your head

# Finding the right word 3

Act the word out

**Target Thinking and Speaking in Primary Schools – 3 Finding the Right Words**

 6

# Finding the right word

## Make your own target card

 8

# Finding the right word

## Make your own target card

5

# Finding the right word

 Draw a picture of the word

7

# Finding the right word

## Make your own target card

# Speaking in Sentences

*'If there is no grammar, there can be no effective communication, it is as simple as that.'*
David Crystal

Speaking in sentences allows children to 'think out loud' and communicate complex thoughts with precision. Children use sentences in a wide range of ways. For example, when telling a story, discussing their ideas in conversation and when commenting on what others say.

Speaking in sentences is part of the process of thinking and speaking:

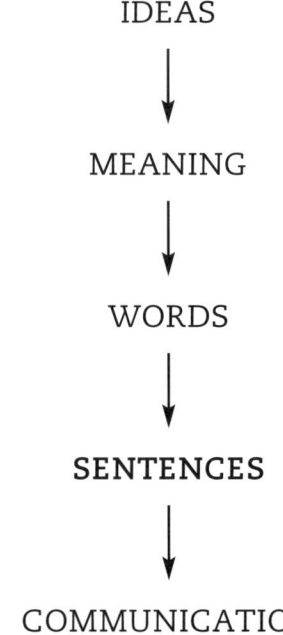

IDEAS

↓

MEANING

↓

WORDS

↓

**SENTENCES**

↓

COMMUNICATION

Sentences are made up of words, and although individual words have meaning, it is only when they are within a sentence that their full meaning is apparent.

The words we choose for our sentence have both **grammar and meaning**. Effective speakers are skilled in both **grammar and meaning**.

# Sentence grammar

The 'grammar' of a sentence is the rule of how it is structured and it has two parts; syntax and morphology.

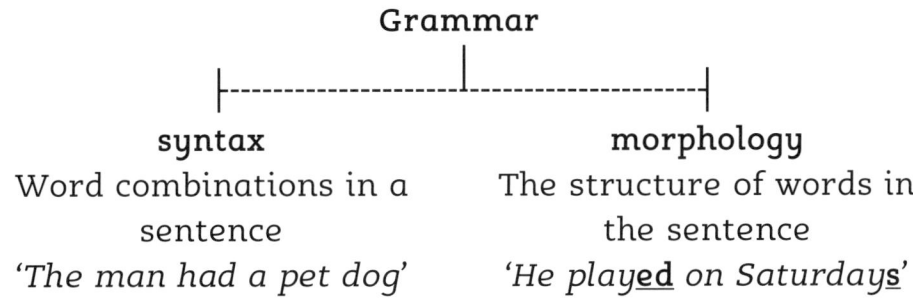

Children learn that a difference in grammar can still convey the same meaning, for example:

- The teacher gave the book to Robert. (an **active verb** 'gave to')
- The book was given to Robert by the teacher. (a **passive verb**, 'was given by')

Children also learn that a difference in grammar is needed to change a statement to a question, for example:

- She ate all her lunch.
- Did she eat all her lunch?

# Sentence meaning

The meaning of the sentence is the result of its grammar plus the meaning of the words within it.

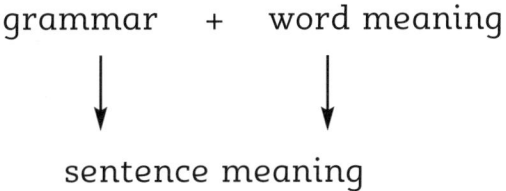

Children learn meaning can be affected by differences in word order, for example:

- Ellie invited Sally to play.
- Sally invited Ella to play.

The meaning of a sentence can also be altered by the speech, rate, rhythm, stress and intonation that is added when we speak.

- That's <u>my</u> book. (and no one else's!)

- That's my <u>book</u>. (not my pen)

# Discourse

'Discourse' is sentences spoken in sequence in a narrative or conversation. It is sentences at their most complex level and involves working memory, keeping track of story lines and building on what has gone before. Sentences used in discourse will show that previous information has been understood, so avoiding unnecessary repetition of information within sentences.

The example demonstrates what information is omitted as being 'redundant' as more sentences are added.

Words in (bold) are those which are left out while the child is speaking.

'On Saturday afternoon I rode my bike all the way from my house to Jack's (house) to play football. When I got there (to Jack's house) he (Jack) wasn't home. I wondered if he had forgotten (about meeting after lunch), but he's usually reliable. So I had a think (about the situation) and went off to the park. Guess what? (happened/ I found). He was there (at the park) getting some extra practice in.

'How you doing?' I said.

(I'm doing) 'Fine' he said.

# Speaking and writing in sentences

The style of sentences is different in spoken and written forms of the language. Historically, written language used to reflect how English was spoken. This is no longer the case so children have to learn both the spoken and written form of the language.

# How sentences develop

Learning to speak in sentences takes time. The child needs to talk with others, practise using the grammar and gauge if it gets his meaning across.

Many children say their **first words** by the time they are **12 months old**. The words are recognised as people or things that are important in the child's life. This is a child's first 'sentence' even though it is only one word long.

**12 months**    *'mama' 'bird' 'bye'*

**By two years** of age a child will usually **join words together** to make longer sentences. The words he chooses show more complex thinking.

**2 years**    *'byebye bird' 'daddy no go'*

By three years of age many children are adding detail to words to indicate precise meaning, for example, plurals 'cats', and past tenses 'jumped'. This is **morphology**.

**3 years** *'Go in the bin'. 'I want more twiglets'. 'He's at work still'.*

**By five years of age**, most children are **joining sentences** with connectives, such as 'if, or, where'. This allows him to relate events in order. A wider range of 'morphology' is used so he is able to communicate his meaning with ever increasing accuracy.

**5 years** *'We were playing on the hill and she was carrying me and she must have dropped me'.*

*'You see that white van Mummy, who's going down the road, the one with the black door at the back, well he's probably going 40 miles an hour and that's too fast'.*

Through his **primary years**, a child learns to express **complex ideas** through sentence grammar. A sentence can be complex without being long.

**5-11 years** *'You should have seen it.' 'Avoid it at all costs.'*

# Normal development of morphology

Morphology is the way words are constructed with beginnings (prefixes) and endings (suffixes) to add to the meaning.

Its development is dependent on such factors as; vocabulary, sentence, and speech development.

The most important aspects of morphology are listed below. They develop between 2 and 7 years of age.

| | |
|---|---|
| /-ing/ verb – present continuous | hitt**ing** |
| plurals | boy**s** |
| /-ed/ verb – past tense | push**ed** |
| /-en/ verb – past participle | brok**en** |
| /-s/ 3rd person singular | eat**s** |
| /-s/ possessive | Jack**'s** |
| /-n't/ negative contracted | isn't |
| Verb 'to be' in contracted form | He**'s** funny. I**'m** hot. |
| /-'s/ contracted verb auxiliary | she**'s** dancing |
| /-est/ superlative | bigg**est** |
| /-er/ comparative | bigg**er** |
| /-ly/ adverb suffix | slow**ly** |

NB The generalisation of morphological rules is a positive sign, e.g. *'foots'*, *'goodest'*, *'sleeped'*, *'runned'*, in the development of a child's spoken grammar, because it demonstrates the child has understood and applied the rule.

Interestingly children may have used the irregular form, *'feet'*, *'best'*, *'slept'*, *'ran'* for a while, then realise the rule and apply it across the board. Most children then go on to learn or re-learn when to use irregular forms.

# Help with speaking in sentences

## Teacher strategies

Do:

- Model correct grammar for the child to hear. Rephrase his sentence if it was incorrect.
  This will reinforce correct usage

- Explain how changing a word (or part of a word) in a sentence alters meaning.
  This gives the child alternatives and possibilities he might not have realised.

- Explain how changing the order of words in a sentence alters meaning. Act out the sentence.
  This shows the child how order of words is important for meaning.

- Practise a new grammatical structure in work activities and then reinforce it in everyday conversation.
  Practising is a good way to learn and remember something new.

- Practise changing statements to questions.
  Asking questions helps thinking and reflection.

- Teach the difference between spoken and written language.
  The rules may need to be taught explicitly.

- Reinforce word endings by highlighting them in written words.
  A visual support can give meaning to verbal information.

- Practise with the child, adding word endings to spoken words. In this way the child learns how speech indicates grammar, for example: walk – walk*ed* (t), open – open*ed* (d), roast*ed* (id).
  When the child hears himself saying the word endings he can begin to understand them.

- Use a tape recorder to teach self-monitoring and self-correction.
  Tape record the child speaking and let him point out improvements.

- Give the child a 'lead in' sentence or phrase if he is stuck with how to begin.
  This will help him to get started.

- Give a specific model of what the child can say.
  This will encourage a response.

- Describe what the child has done well, for example, 'you remembered all the past tenses in your story'.
  This positive feedback focuses on their success.

- Give the child a sentence and ask him to say the same idea in a different way.
  This helps the child express his meaning flexibly using different sentence structures.

# Help with speaking in sentences

## Child strategies

- **Take time to think of your sentence.**
  You will become quicker the more you practise.

- **Make a picture in your head of what you want to say.**
  This can help you focus on what is happening and so help you to start your sentence.

- **Think of the verb (doing word) for your sentence and then add the other words to it.**
  Verbs are the most important part of a sentence and a good place to start your thinking.

- **Join your sentences by using a connective. Use the ones on the next page.**
  This is a way of joining your ideas together.

- **Say your sentence out loud before you write it.**
  This is a way of checking your sentence.

## Connectives

| and | because | so | then |
|---|---|---|---|
| and then | but | or | if |
| unless | although | who | in spite of |

## Connectives of time and sequence

| at first | until | before |
|---|---|---|
| after | next | later on |
| when | while | a bit later |
| soon | now | after a while |
| finally | eventually | |

## Word Order

1. Look at the picture. Discuss what's happening.

2. Cut up each sentences into its phrases.

3. The child moves the phrases to make a sentence.

4. Next cut the sentences up into its words.

5. The child moves the words around to make a sentence.

- Ellie | stepped | forward | and | pushed | the boat | gently | towards the water.

- The boat | hit | the water | with a splash.

- The tidal wave | gave | the frogs | a fright.

- The boat | bobbed | happily | up and down | on the water.

- Ellie | smiled | and | looked | very | pleased | with herself.

*Cont'd*

From 'Pitt Street Pirates' – Terry Deary

# Connectives

Use a connective and then complete these sentences.

**Version 1**

but     then     finally     because     meanwhile     however

1. The football team won their match ..........
2. The tortoise won the race ............
3. They climbed the mountain all day, ............
4. It took them five hours to finish the garden ...
5. To make porridge add milk and water to oats......
6. To make this activity easier write a whole sentence but leave out the connecting word.
   For example, 'Ben got wet _____ it was raining.

**Version 2**

Make a sentence starting with these connectives.

1. Because of the storm .......
2. Although he ........
3. In spite of feeling ill ......
4. At first .........
5. Eventually ............

**Version 3**

1. Pick a connective.
2. Join two of your own sentences using the connective.

# Retelling a story

**Act out the following story for the child using miniature toys as props.**

It's Sam's birthday party. He <u>writes</u> invitations and <u>sends</u> them to his friends. Charlie <u>gets</u> his invitation and <u>drives</u> to the party in his car. Billy <u>rides</u> to the party on his bike. Tom is so excited he <u>runs</u> all the way. Charlie, Bill and Tom <u>give</u> Sam lots of presents. Sam <u>says</u> 'Thank you'.

Sam's mum <u>brings</u> in a big chocolate cake with candles on. They all sing 'Happy Birthday' to Sam. Sam <u>blows</u> out the candles and <u>sits</u> down with his friends. At the end of the day Sam <u>says</u> 'bye' to everyone. That night Sam <u>feels</u> tired and <u>sleeps</u> very well.

1. Retell the story using the past tense. All the <u>underlined verbs</u> change to an irregular past tense.

2. Ask the child to retell the story.

3. To make it easier to remember, take turns to tell the next step of the story.

Use the bingo squares on this page as the board.

| slept | swam | ate | drove |
|-------|------|-----|-------|
| wrote | got up | drew | thought |

| woke up | sat | knew | crept |
|---------|-----|------|-------|
| told | came | held | drank |

*Cont'd*

Use these sheets to photocopy and cut up to put on the bingo boards on the previous page.

| | | | |
|---|---|---|---|
| sleep | swim | eat | drive |
| write | get up | draw | think |

| | | | |
|---|---|---|---|
| wake up | sit | know | creep |
| tell | come | hold | drink |

## Spot the Mistake

1. The sentences can be read out loud by the child or the adult.

2. Ask if the child can hear what is wrong and suggest how to say it correctly.

3. Some children will not be aware the sentence is incorrect. They will need help to understand the underlying grammar.

4. Writing the sentence can support your explanation of what is incorrect. It can help the child to focus on listening to the incorrect part. This may not be possible, however, if the child is not yet able to read.

*Sentences:*

1. After she stopped the car, the lady will get out.

2. As the audience cheered, Wayne singed.

3. Has you seen my mobile phone?

4. Yesterday I watch TV and phoned my friend.

5. We have eat lunch already.

6. Stop right here and waiting for me to catch up.

7. I is been working really hard today.

8. How many of those burgers does you want?

9. Since I am 6 years old I have played the guitar.

10. Could you be quiet? I am trying to work.

# Joining Verb Phrases

1  Cut up the verb phrases and mix the words up.

2  Ask the child to put the correct preposition with its verb.

3  Explain any difficulties.

4  Use these verb phrases in spoken and written sentences.

| **think** | *about* | **carry** | *on* |
|-----------|---------|-----------|------|
| **drink** | *up* | **look** | *for* |
| **head** | *for* | **sit** | *down* |
| **clear** | *away* | **look** | *at* |

**2** 🎯

Start sentences sometimes with these connectives:

Although …

Because …

Unless …

**4** 🎯

Past tenses prompt:

sleep > slept

.............. >

.............. >

.............. >

.............. >

**1** 🎯

Use these connectives in a story sequence:

first/at first

next/and then

finally/last

**3** 🎯

I am working to say

..............................

..............................

Target Thinking and Speaking in Primary Schools – 4 Speaking in Sentences
© J Reilly & S Murray 2005: this may be reproduced for class use solely within the purchaser's school or college

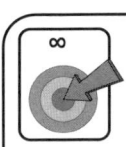

## Verb Phrases:

6

| think about | carry on | look out |
| drink up | look for | head for |
| sit down | clear away | look at |

..........

..........

## Make your own target card

5

# Use powerful verbs in your speaking

'heaving, raising, straining, grunting'

7

## Make your own target card

## Make your own target card

# Speaking Clearly

*Andrew: 'He's sPurPing''. Marcus: 'No, its slurTing.'*
*(slurping)*

Note, in this chapter <u>speech sounds</u> are denoted within //
as in the <u>sound</u> /f/. This is distinct from the written <u>letter</u>
which is indicated using ' ' as in 'f'.

This chapter deals with the different skills a child needs
in order to speak clearly. Being able to speak clearly
enables a child to engage with others and be understood
by them. This, in turn, is central to the development of
thinking skills.

A child who cannot speak clearly may struggle to get his
ideas across. This can lead to frustration and sometimes
aggressive or withdrawn behaviour.

## Making and organising speech sounds

Speech sounds are **made** when the lips, tongue, teeth, air
and vocal cords move in different combinations. For
example, the sound /p/ is made by the lips closing, and
with air from the lungs, while the sound /t/ is made by
the tip of the tongue touching behind the top teeth, and
with air from the lungs. How sounds are made is called
**articulation**.

How we **organise** these speech sounds affects the meaning
of a word. This is called **phonology**. A change in speech
sound changes meaning, e.g. /pea, tea/ and the way we
sequence sounds also changes meaning, e.g. /top, pot/.

# Speech sound development

This is a process that has certainly begun by the time a child is born. He will experiment with many speech, and non-speech sounds during his first year.

A child begins to say his first recognisable words at around twelve months. At this point he is learning **how** to make sounds including /m/, /a/, /d/. He is also learning how these sounds are organised to mean useful words such as /mama/ /dada/ to mean 'Mummy' and 'Daddy'.

Gradually the non-speech sounds are dropped from his repertoire as he learns which ones are important for the language he is using.

A child practises and experiments with speech sounds throughout his pre-school years. For example he will play with sounds to create rhymes. By the time he goes to school, he will be understood by his teachers and classmates.

Children are still learning **how** to say some speech sounds when they go to school, such as /th/ and /r/ which are the last speech sounds to be mastered. Some speech sound combinations will be mastered during the first few years of school. They are complex consonant blends such as /scr, thr, spl/. These sounds require precise control *and* co-ordination of lips, tongue, teeth, air and vocal cords.

# Usual development of speech sounds (taken from PACS, P. Grunwell, 1982)

Sounds develop from those made at the front of the mouth, /b, p, m/ to those made at the back, /k,g, ng/

They develop from the most simple movement /p/ to complex and co-ordinated movement, /scr, thr/.

The general order in which the sounds develop is described below, though there may be considerable differences between individual children.

By 24 months  /b,m,d,p,t,n,w/

24–36 months  /f,s,k,g,y,h/

3–4½ years  /v,z,sh,j,l/
/sp,st,sc,sm,sn/
/bl,cl,fl,gl,pl,sl/

4 to 8 years  /spr,skr, str, skw/
/th, r, thr/

# Individual differences

Different children develop their speech sounds at different *rates*. However, there is a general order in which sounds usually develop. From the easiest to make, usually /m, d, p/ to the most difficult /th/ at 7 or 8 years of age, there is considerable variation between children.

Some children find it hard to 'hear' the difference between /f, v, th/ and do not realise that /th/ is a separate sound. It is also a difficult sound to make as it requires good control of the tongue.

(In some dialects it is appropriate to use /f/ instead of /th/. They may say /f/ in words such as '<u>th</u>ink' – so saying '<u>f</u>ink').

Other children may take a long time to say the sound /y/ and say /l/ instead so saying '<u>l</u>ellow' instead of '<u>y</u>ellow'.

Adults may notice a single speech sound a child cannot say and use, whilst overlooking the fact he has developed all the other speech sounds without difficulty.

# Speech rhythm, rate, intonation and stress

Rhythm, intonation and stress also carry meaning when we speak. This also has to be learnt in order to speak clearly.

- A different **rhythm** is used when saying a nursery rhyme to speaking in conversation.
- The **rate** of speech changes according to the situation. We might speak quickly when we are in a hurry to get information across. We might speak slowly to catch someone's attention.
- A rising **intonation** is used in a question, 'What did you say?', while a falling intonation can be used to

emphasise agreement with someone's opinion, 'Agreed!'

- The **stress** of a word can tell us about its meaning in a sentence, for example, verb 'to be up<u>set</u>', noun 'an <u>up</u>set'. A child will need to use the correct stress pattern as well as the correct sound combination in a word e.g., /under<u>stand</u>/, /<u>off</u>icer/.

# Speaking clearly and literacy skills

Speech and literacy skills are closely linked. There can be serious repercussions in literacy attainment if a child cannot speak clearly.

A child with speech difficulties may not be able to work out the phonology (organisation) of the sounds of the written language and may be found to be dyslexic.

**When spelling**, a child says the word, breaks it down into its individual sounds (phonemes), then matches the speech sounds to the letters (graphemes). The child has to say the word accurately in order to break it down accurately.

A child who says a word incorrectly is likely to spell it as he says it, for example 'wi<u>v</u>' instead of 'wi<u>th</u>'.

**When reading**, the child says the sound for each letter then blends them together in the right order to say the word. A child who has problems organising sounds may struggle to blend them in the right order for example /t/, /o/, /p/, which he may blend together as 'pot'.

Accurate reading may be difficult to achieve if the child cannot match the letters to sounds. Reading comprehension will be affected too. This can mean reading is a laborious and unrewarding activity.

During the school years, speech and literacy interact and develop together. The skills of the teacher, and speech and language therapist should therefore support and complement one another.

# The skills children need in order to speak clearly:

- a clear speech model
- normal hearing during the years that speech sounds are learnt
- the ability to discriminate between sounds
- an understanding of how sounds are organised, in other words which sounds are important to the language used
- the ability to use and co-ordinate lips, tongue, teeth, air and vocal cords at speed
- encouragement to speak even if speech is not always clear
- the opportunity to talk and practise speech sounds

# Difficulties in speaking clearly

A child may not be able to speak clearly because he cannot make (articulate) the speech sounds, because he does not know how speech sounds are organised (phonology), or both (articulation and phonology). An assessment by a speech and language therapist will ascertain which is the case.

It is important to find out the nature of the child's speech difficulty, because working on articulation when there are phonological difficulties is counterproductive and could be damaging.

A speech difficulty can affect a child's ability to access information from memory when thinking of ideas. The link between the word meaning and the sound of the word may be weak. Therefore retrieval of the word will be weak.

A speech difficulty may result in the child being unable to pronounce word morphology such as past tenses, /slep<u>t</u>/ plurals, /cat<u>s</u>/. This requires automatic and fast articulation.

Stammering may affect clarity and use of speech sounds as can some drugs which can induce slurring in speech.

In all these cases intervention is more than just targeting clear speech.

# Knowing when to intervene

Isolated speech sound substitutions should be viewed in perspective. If the child has developed all other speech sounds appropriately, it is reasonable to think he will learn to say all sounds clearly in time.

If the sound substitution does not interfere with communication and is consistent with the child's age, speech and language therapy is not appropriate, as in this example, from a six year old. *'His little brother's only aged free'* (three).

If, on the other hand, a child is distressed and frustrated by his or her inability to speak clearly, referral to a speech and language therapist is appropriate. For example, a ten year old who says his /s/ sounds with the air inappropriately coming out of the side of the mouth, a slushy 's', and is distressed or teased because of his speech.

The child's speech should be viewed in relation to that of his speech community. If the family come from Liverpool, for example, they will articulate some sounds in a different way, for example /k/ at the end of some words.

Different communities use vowels in different ways in their dialect. It is important to understand what usage is normal for the community before making judgements regarding intervention.

Most speech sound difficulties concern the consonants; however some children have difficulty saying vowel sounds. If this is the case, their speech difficulty is likely to be more severe and long standing. The advice of a speech and language therapist should be sought for these children.

Difficulties with speech rate, intonation, stress and rhythm can often be due to other language difficulties. Concerns regarding these areas should lead to a referral to a speech and language therapist.

Hearing should be routinely checked whenever there are concerns about a child's speech.

# Help with speaking clearly

Remediation of speech difficulties is complex.

The strategies suggested are those which are reasonable for a teacher to incorporate within the school curriculum and the classroom.

Neither teachers nor classroom assistants should feel they must take on the role of the speech and language therapist in helping children who do not speak clearly. However they might feel they can carry out specific speech work for a particular child in collaboration with the child's speech and language therapist.

## Teacher strategies

Do:

- **Listen to the child and tell him you value his effort to speak.**
  A child will continue to make an effort if he is rewarded/acknowledged.

- **Slow down the rate at which you talk to the child.**
  This can allow the child time to process speech sounds and therefore make more sense of it.

- **Check that the child is hearing normally.**
  Suggest a hearing test if you think he is not hearing normally.

- **Plot the child's speech sound development on the Speech Development Chart.**
  This information can help you decide if a referral to a Speech and Language Therapist is appropriate.

- **Be aware of the local dialect of the child or the dialect spoken at home. This will influence which sounds are considered appropriate to use.**
  Children will use the speech sounds of their family and peers so they are not alienated from them.

- **Keep a close check on literacy development, especially the use of phonic strategies in reading and spelling.**
  Good phonology is needed for blending and segmentation.

- **Clap out the correct number of the syllables of multisyllabic words.**
  The child may not be aware of the correct number of syllables.

- **Point out the weakest and strongest syllables in multisyllabic words.**
  The weakest syllable is the hardest to hear and is the shortest too. For example, in the word 'computer' 'com' is the weakest syllable and hardest to hear. This is why some children say 'puter'.

- **Highlight tricky parts of the word.**
  This can make the child aware of parts of the word he finds difficult to say.

- **Cut tricky words up into syllables.**
  Building up from syllables is easier than individual sounds in the word.

- **Choose a small number of everyday words to work on, which contain the difficult sound.**
  Everyday words allow for practice and are relevant to the child.

- **If the child is receiving speech and language therapy find out what strategies for support have been suggested by the therapist.**
  Using a strategy will give him the opportunity for practice and build his confidence.

- **For a child whose speech is very unclear, suggest two alternative words for the child to choose from to narrow down what he is trying to say.**
  This can be a useful strategy for the teacher and the child.

- **Repeat back slowly the correct pronunciation for the word or phrase.**
  It is important the child hears a good model when his attempt is always incorrect.

- **Avoid repeating back to the child his incorrect pronunciation.**
  This will add to the child's distress and will not help him to change his pronunciation.

- **If the child can read, show them how the sounds are represented in the written word.**
  This can help some children to see the difference between what they say and how a word should be pronounced.

- Some children who hear and use different accents and languages at home and at school can find this confusing.

  Hearing different accents at home and at school can be confusing for some children and they may need more time to develop their speech sound system.

- Be sensitive to those children who are embarrassed by their speech difficulty. Use phrases such as 'I am sorry I am finding it hard to understand you. Can you say it again for me?'

  This will show the child that what he has to say is valued.

- Respond to what the child says rather than *how* he says it.

  The child's ideas are the most important.

- Use alternative strategies to support children whose speech is not clear.

  Use gestures, pictures, the written word etc., in order to keep communication open.

- Allow mime and acting out as alternatives to speaking.

  This can take the pressure off the child to speak yet allows the child to communicate.

- Devise a personal book of difficult words that have pictures or the written words.

  This book can act as a personal reference for the child to use when stuck.

- If the child's speech remains difficult to understand or he is distressed by it, discuss a referral to a speech and language therapist with his parents.

  The speech and language therapist is trained to assess and treat this kind of difficulty.

# Help with speaking clearly

## Child strategies

- **Find alternative ways to get your meaning across,** for example, draw a picture or write the word or use a gesture or mime what you want to say.
  This can make speaking easier for you.

- **Use other words to get your meaning across.**
  Have a bank of useful words that you can say clearly and stick with them.

- **Clap out the number of syllables of the word.**
  This may give the other person a clue which could make it less frustrating for you both.

- **It's OK not to speak if you are embarrassed.**
  Agree on this with the teacher so you are not constantly worried about being asked to speak.

- **Use strategies the speech and language therapist has taught you.**
  Strategies become more automatic when you practise them.

# Correct consonant sounds in English

These are the correct common speech sounds for spoken English. Some of the **sounds** are written using a **single letter**, e.g. 'p'. Some sounds are written using **two letters**, e.g. 'sh'. Some sounds can be written in more than one way e.g. /j/ as in **'judge'**.

| | | | |
|---|---|---|---|
| p | as in pie | v | as in violin |
| b | as in ball | sh | as in shop |
| t | as in tie | s | as in measure |
| d | as in dog | ch | as in chin |
| k | as in king and cat | j | as in judge |
| g | as in garden | y | as in you |
| m | as in man | w | as in water |
| n | as in nut | l | as in leg |
| ng | as in sing | ll | as in fell |
| s | as in sun | r | as in robin |
| z | as in zebra | h | as in house |
| f | as in four | th | as in think |
| th | as in this | | |

1. Talk about each word; what it means and how to say it.

2. Work out which syllable has the strongest beat. Highlight or underline it.

3. Ask the child to draw a picture for it or visualise it. This can help with understanding and remembering.

4. Cut up the words you want to use with the child.

5. Say the word syllable by syllable/ take turns to say syllables.

6. Add words to the list that the child finds difficult.

7. Make sure you talk about both the *meaning and structure* of the word.

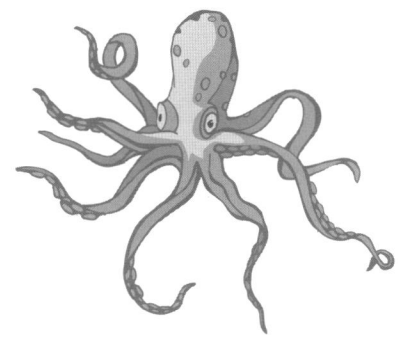

| oc | to | pus |
|----|----|-----|

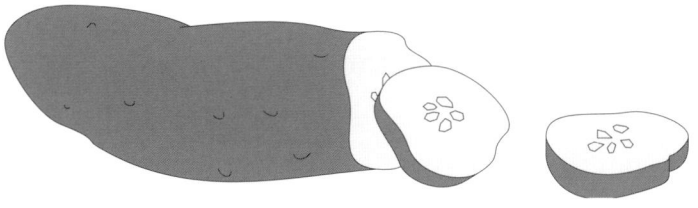

| cu | cum | ber |
|----|-----|-----|

*Cont'd*

| rhi | noc | er | os |
|-----|-----|-----|-----|

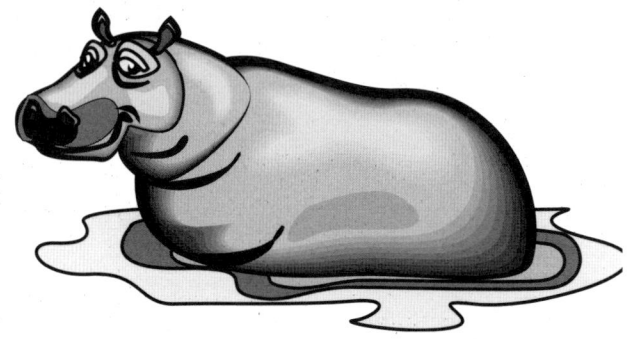

| hip | po | pot | a | mus |
|-----|-----|-----|-----|-----|

Other words to use with a picture are:

3 syllables: potato, tangerine, dinosaur

4 syllables: cauliflower, avocado, diplodocus

5 syllables: tyrannosaurus, vegetarian, inspirational

## Listening for Mistakes in a Rhyme

1. Choose a common rhyme or story appropriate to the child.

2. Change key familiar words in the story and ask the child to listen for the incorrect word.

3. Tell the child how many words to listen out for, for example, one mistake every two lines.

---

Humpty Dumpty sat on a wall

Humpty Dumpty had a great **ball** (fall)

All the King's horses and all the King's men

Couldn't put **Bumpty** (Humpty) together again.

---

*Choose stories such as:*

Horrid Henry

Tracy Beaker stories

Harry Potter stories

Lion King

A Series of Unfortunate Events by Lemony Snicket

Barrington Stoke fiction

---

## Learning to use Complex Words at Speed

1   Choose a familiar story in which the characters and place names are well known to the child.

2   Breaking the words down into syllables as in the **Word Puzzles** activity 5:1 where words and pictures are used.

3   Practise saying the words at increasing speed. If the child becomes inaccurate, ask them to say the words more slowly. *Accuracy must always come before speed.*

4   Once the single word is correct at normal conversational speed, put it into a sentence.

5   Make a story from the sentences using **connectives**.

### Lion King:

| Simba | Pride Lands | Mufasa | Sarabi |
|---|---|---|---|
| wilde beest | Zazu | Banzai | Shenzi |
| Timon | Pride Rock | Scar | Queen Nala |
| Rafiki | Circle of Life | kingdom | Pumbah |

# *Alliteration*

1. Make up sentences using nouns, verbs, adjectives and adverbs, all starting with the same sound.

2. For those children who find this activity difficult use colour-coded parts of speech, for example Sentifix™ bricks by Philip and Tacey.

| adjective + noun | verb | noun | adverb |
|---|---|---|---|
| Angry Arthur | ate | apples | angrily. |
| Bored Ben | bounced | balls | beautifully. |

| Question | verb | noun | adverb |
|---|---|---|---|
| Can you | catch | cans | carefully? |
| Do you | drop | dragons | dangerously? |
| Would you | wash | Wellingtons | willingly? |

This activity is also good for speaking in sentences – see chapter 4.

## Miming

This can be played with one child or with a small group of children.

1. Cut out the words and stick them onto cards.

2. Talk to the child or children about the meaning of the words.

3. Mime (act out) the words. Be inventive and whacky!

4. Put all the pictures in a pile.

5. The child takes a picture and mimes it for the others to guess.

6. Whoever guesses correctly takes the next card.

7. Play the same game using words for everyday objects or words the child finds difficult to say.

calculator

pomegranate

hospital

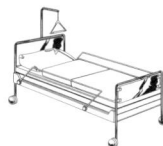

Cinema

escalator

glockenspiel

tagliatelle          encyclopaedia          parallelogram          interactive whiteboard

## Using Poetry to Help Speech and Rhythm

1. Choose a poem or rhyme with a regular rhythm. Some children will find it easier to keep pace using a rhyme.

2. Tape the poem.

3. Tap or clap out the rhythm whilst listening to the tape. Then let the child have a turn.

4. Allow the child to join in with the tape when he is ready.

5. The syllables in **bold and underlined** are the strongest/stressed syllables.

From 'Slinky Malinki' by Lynley Dodd

**<u>Sli</u>**nky Ma**<u>lin</u>**ki

was **<u>bla</u>**cker than **<u>black</u>**,

a **<u>stal</u>**king and **<u>lur</u>**king

Ad**<u>ven</u>**turous **<u>cat</u>**.

He had **<u>bright</u>** **<u>yell</u>**ow **<u>eyes</u>**,

a **<u>warb</u>**ling **<u>wail</u>**

and a **<u>kink</u>** at the **<u>end</u>**

of his **<u>very</u>** **<u>long</u>** **<u>tail</u>**.

## Words I am learning to say:

## Words I am saying faster:

## Words I am using in sentences when I speak and write:

| nouns | verbs | adjectives | adverbs |
|-------|-------|------------|---------|
|       |       |            |         |
|       |       |            |         |
|       |       |            |         |

## Phrases and sentences I am practising saying clearly:

1

2

3

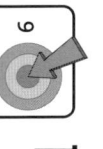

# Make your own target card

# Make your own target card

# Make your own target card

# Make your own target card

# Thinking and Speaking in Conversation

'To understand another's speech, it is not sufficient to understand his words – we must understand his thought.'
Vygotsky

## Conversation is a complex activity

When thinking and speaking come together in conversation, the child is managing a complex and integrated system of skills. In conversation, the child takes the dual roles of speaker **and** listener, alternating between the two. Thinking, (along with understanding), connects the two roles.

All the skills described in the chapters of this book come together in conversation.

The mind can be thinking of many different and diverse ideas at the same time. However, only one idea at a time can be conveyed through speaking. These ideas are given meaning when they are put into words and communicated in conversation.

Thinking and speaking have been separated for the purpose of the book when describing the skills needed for each. However they co-occur and there is two-way interaction between the two skills.

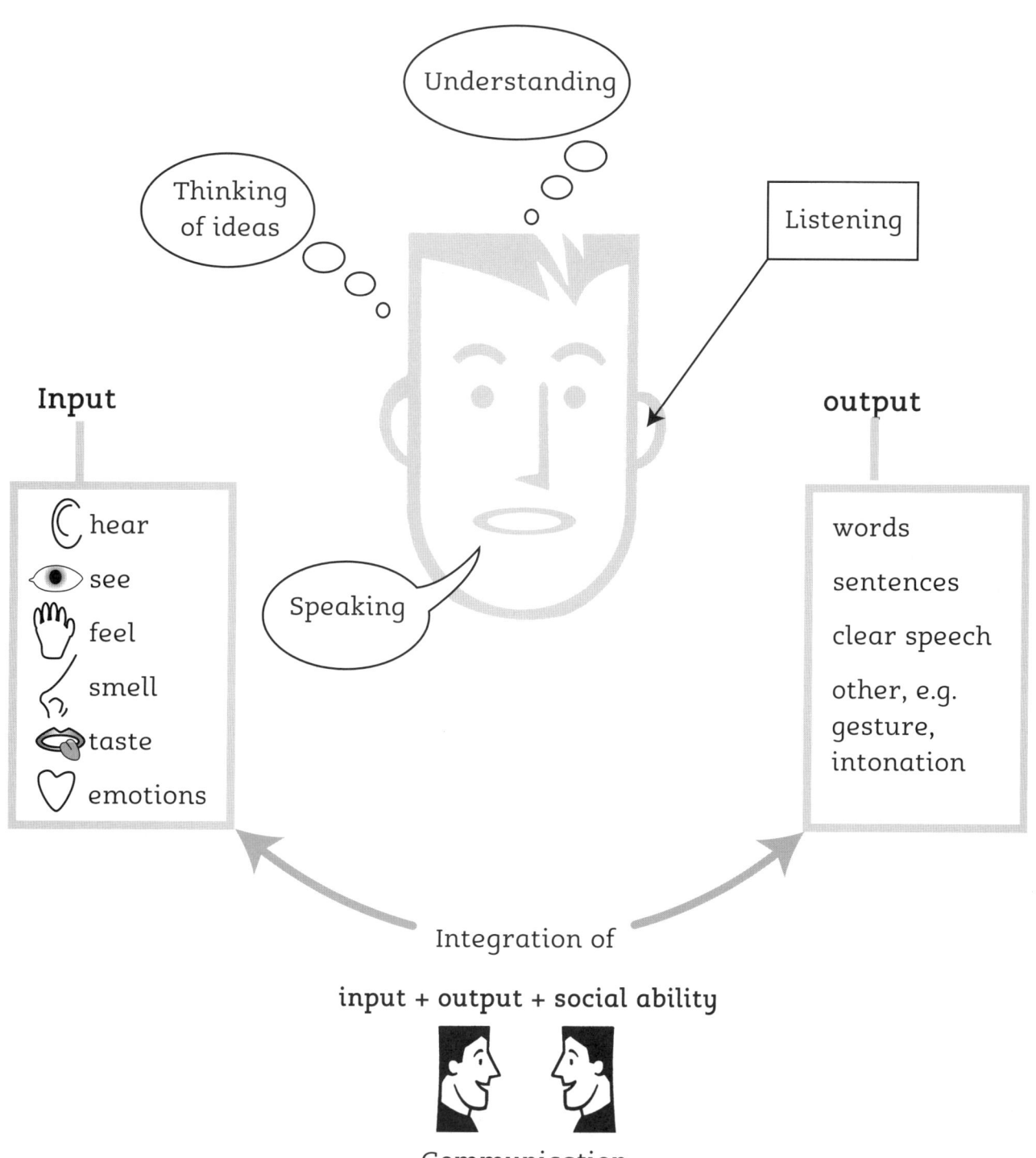

**Input**

- hear
- see
- feel
- smell
- taste
- emotions

**output**

- words
- sentences
- clear speech
- other, e.g. gesture, intonation

Thinking of ideas

Understanding

Listening

Speaking

Integration of

input + output + social ability

Communication

# Conversation as a social activity

A child engages in conversation to socialise with others, to build friendships and to share ideas. A competent thinker and speaker is aware of how he relates to others. He has empathy with other people and understands they have feelings, thoughts and needs too.

In conversation, a child shows an interest in the other person's point of view. At the same time he thinks about *his* point of view and how to get it across. He takes turns to speak. He listens to and thinks about what the other person says.

While he is engaged in conversation a child is monitoring what the other person is saying. He uses his senses to pick up information so he can adjust, and 'repair' the conversation if there are misunderstandings. He is tuned into verbal information (e.g. words) and non-verbal information (e.g. body language) and processes both simultaneously.

To think and speak in a group the child needs to collaborate with others and understand their feelings and needs.

Children who are good at thinking and speaking in conversation are likely to build friendships easily and feel confident in group situations.

Children who have difficulty engaging in conversation will probably feel isolated and confused. They will find it difficult to contribute to group discussion as this requires rapid and flexible thinking and speaking.

# Different styles of conversation

A child will use different styles of conversation according to the situation and the person he is speaking to. For example, one moment he may be chatting to a friend and the next speaking to the teacher. He needs to be able to switch easily and quickly between the two and converse appropriately with both. The child who cannot make this switch easily or is unaware of the need to do so, will come across as socially inappropriate.

He needs to work out:

- Which language style to use. For example, he needs to be more polite when talking to his teacher than to his friend.
- Which words are appropriate to use with each. For example, his friend could think him odd if he referred to his mobile as a telephone.
- What information to share. For example, saying he was bored would be fine to say to a friend but not to a guest speaker.
- What non-verbal clues to use. For example, it would not be appropriate for him to sigh heavily during assembly!
- When and if to interrupt. For example, it could be appropriate for him to interrupt a friend telling him a joke if he had heard it ten times before.

# Thinking and speaking in conversation

To think and speak in conversation a child co-ordinates a vast range of skills which include:

- selecting a topic
- sticking to the topic
- finding the right words
- putting sentences together
- taking turns and handing turns on
- adapting to the audience and situation
- using non-verbal signals to reinforce his meaning
- judging if he has been understood and repairing misunderstandings

All this happens at great speed, simultaneously and automatically. In addition to thinking and speaking, the child is also performing the complex task of listening and understanding.

# Difficulties in thinking and speaking in conversation

There are many skills that work together when a child is thinking and speaking effectively in conversation. Difficulties may occur because the child has difficulty in **any one or more** of the skills described in the book. Alternatively, he may have difficulty integrating skills together at the **speed** needed for effective communication.

In conversation, interaction between those taking part, is continually changing. Its success relies on each person understanding the rules and abiding by them.

Rita Jordan and Stuart Powell, (1995) describe the difficulties that children with autism experience in conversation; *'like trying to learn a complicated dance, when you do not know what dancing is, when you cannot hear the music, and when, just as you have managed to imitate one step of your partner's, you find that the dance has moved on, the rhythm has changed and so (perhaps) has your partner.'*

This analogy of a conversation being like a dance can be applied to many children who have difficulty thinking and speaking in conversation, even when they do not have autism.

When considering how to help a child it is important to look at all the individual skills for thinking and speaking, as well as how they are integrated.

# Help with thinking and speaking in conversation

*Teacher strategies*

**Do:**

- **Tell the child what the topic is. Remind him to stick to the topic.**
  This will help keep his thoughts and ideas relevant.

- **Teach the thinking and speaking skills which conversation relies on.**
  Difficulties shown in conversation often relate back to weaknesses in thinking and speaking.

- **Teach the meaning of non-verbal communication. For example, how to use body language and facial expression to show an interest in what another person is saying.**
  Children may not learn these skills automatically.

- **Practise turn-taking in conversation.**
  This will develop the child's skills as a listener and speaker.

- **Tell the child when he has said enough.**
  He may not know how to judge this himself.

- **Recap what the child has said during his turn.**
  This teaches relevance and conciseness.

- **Teach the child to review what has been said in a discussion.**
  This engages the child in an active way to think.

- **Tell the child when what he says does not fit in with what has gone before.**
  This teaches him about keeping to the topic.

- **Role play conversations about topics and situations relevant to the child.**
  This teaches the child what to say.

- Write stories to explain social situations.
  This makes the underlying rules clear
  For example, Carol Gray's Social Stories. (1994)

# Help with thinking and speaking in conversation

## Child strategies

- **Think about the situation.**
  Am I talking to lots of people or just one?

- **Think about who you are talking to.**
  For example, am I talking to an adult and so need to be extra polite?

- **Ask an adult to write a story to explain the rules of the situation you find confusing.**
  This can help with knowing what to do and say.

- **Watch a person's face and body for information.**
  This adds to the meaning of what to say.

- **Practise the skills used in thinking and speaking.**
  Practising a skill makes it easier and more automatic.

## Asking Questions to Find Out Information

1. Two children face one another with a barrier between them so they cannot see their partner's picture.

2. Both children have the same picture. Start with the one on page 130.

3. The first child puts a cross somewhere on his picture. He does not tell the other child where it is.

4. The second child asks the first child questions in order to find out where the cross has been put. The first child can only ask questions which have the answer 'Yes', or 'No'.

5. If the second child asks a question that cannot be answered 'Yes' or 'No', the first child can say to him 'That isn't the right kind of question'.

6. The second child continues to ask questions until the cross is located accurately.

7. Swap roles.

If a child has difficulty thinking of the right kind of questions, discuss how to start the question so the answer is 'Yes' or 'No'.

**example**

'Is the cross on the ...?

Will I find the cross under the ...?

Can you see the cross somewhere above ...?

**Extension activity**: Use geometric shapes. One child builds a design using different shapes, colours and sizes. The other child has to ask questions to determine which shapes have been used and their arrangement.

*Cont'd*

From 'Ghost for Sale' – Terry Deary

**Target Thinking and Speaking in Primary Schools** – 6 Thinking and Speaking in Conversation

## Round Robin Circle Activities

1    Use the starters below to go round the group asking each child for their contribution.

2    Ensure each child sticks to the topic.

3    Encourage each child to think of different ideas to the ones previously put forward in the group.

# Starters to think about:

- Good toys to play with when a friend comes round........

- My best friend and I like to .........

- Great holiday activities that cost nothing .......

- Things that make me happy ...

- Things that make me mad .......

# More difficult things to think about:

- What if trees were red?

- If you could buy sunshine ............

- What if every day was the weekend?

- How do animals blow out their birthday candles ........... ?

- Your school has been given an old building for the pupils to use as they want.....................

## Stick to the Topic!

Use the topic cards on the next page.

There are two ways to do the activity.

## Version 1:

Pass the topic card round the circle, each saying something about the topic.

## Version 2:

Pass the topic card round the circle.

Each child says something about that topic that builds on what the previous person has said. For example:

| | |
|---|---|
| Speaker 1 | 'Sharks are very **dangerous**.' |
| Speaker 2 | 'I know they are **dangerous**, because people have been **attacked** by sharks.' |
| Speaker 3 | 'Sharks often **attack** people if they panic. It's better to swim quietly away if you see one.' |

*Cont'd*

# Fast food

# Sharks

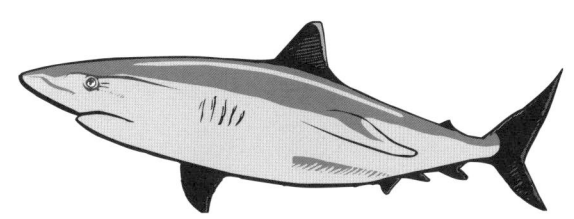

# Homework

# War

# Hobbies

# Holidays

# If I were a slug

# TV

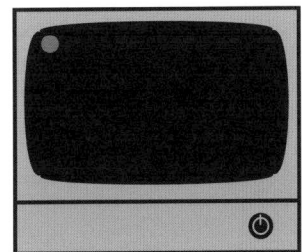

## Role Play

1. Take an everyday situation that could happen in class or the playground, such as children excluding another child from their play.

2. Draw the event on the board. Add speech bubbles to show what each person said. Add thought bubbles to show what each person was thinking. Give each person a feeling based on how he or she felt at the time.

3. Try to get the children to think about each others thoughts and feelings as well as their own. Useful questions might be:

   What did you hear William say?
   Can you picture how Joshua's face looked?
   Why might Emma have said that?
   What might Andrew have been thinking?

4. Act out the event by giving *different* parts to the children involved. This will help them see things from another point of view.

5. Guide them to act out and talk about the consequences of actions.

6. Aim to find a resolution where no-one feels hurt, everyone has been able to put their view across and each child has seen the event from a different perspective.

**1**   Give the children the first two lines of a conversation and ask them to continue it, for example:

      Speaker 1    'Have you got a skateboard?'

      Speaker 2    'You must be joking!'

**2**   Give the last two lines of a conversation and ask the children to provide the first part, for example:

      Speaker 1    Thank goodness we weren't caught.'

      Speaker 2    'I'm never going there again.'

# Extension Activity – Conversation

1. This is an extract from 'Ghost for Sale' by Terry Deary. It is part of a conversation between Mr and Mrs Rundle.

2. Cut out the boxes and ask the child to arrange the conversation in order.

3. Accept what the child has arranged and use it to talk about the importance of following on from what was previously said.

4. Help them to rearrange to a different order if it does not make sense.

---

Mrs Rundle buttoned up her cardigan fiercely. 'There is a large hairy spider crawling up your nose to eat your brain!' she said.

---

'Really, dear?'

---

'But it's run out because it can't find any brains in there.'

---

'Ah, that'll be right dear,' Mr Rundle nodded and turned the page.

---

'I've put poison in your tea,' she went on sweetly.

---

'Good grief!' the man cried suddenly.

---

1   Give the children a topic to discuss for example:

| Mobile Phones | Zoos |
|---|---|
| Watching TV | We are what we eat |
| Going on a field trip | Reading comics |

*Cont'd*

**2** Show the children what makes a good discussion.

| | |
|---|---|
| Listen carefully to what others say.  | Join in. Make thoughtful relevant comments.  |
| Stick to the topic. Be relevant.  | Ask questions to clarify what others mean.  |
| Deal politely with others. Draw others into the conversation.   | **Summarise.**<br><br>● **What were the main points?**<br>● **Is there a conclusion?**<br>● **How did the discussion go?** |

**3** Have a discussion about the topic. It's even better if you can tape or video it and replay it later.

**4** Evaluate the discussion using the sheet on page 139. Either use one sheet for the whole group or give each child a sheet to fill in.

# Discussion evaluation sheet

Topic _____ Date _____

Name _____

Number in the group _____

---

How much did you join in the discussion?

Too much _____

About enough _____

Not enough _____

---

Do you think it was a good discussion?

Yes _____     No _____

Give 2 reasons why?

1. _____

2. _____

---

Write one thing that would have made the discussion better.

_____

---

I would award my performance in the discussion _____ / 10

**2**

# Take turns to talk and listen

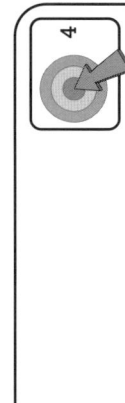

'It's good to talk.'

'And listen.'

---

**1**

# Listen carefully to what others say and then join in.

I like cats too.

---

**4**

# Stick to the topic.
# Talk about the same thing.

---

**3**

# Ask questions to check what others mean.

### e.g. 'What did you mean by that?'

........................................

### This can help you to follow the conversation.

---

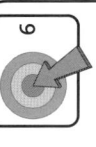

**Ways to start a conversation.**

- Can I play with you?
- That looks like a good game, can I join in?
- I heard you talking about.....

**Deal with misunderstandings.**

'Have you understood?'

**Make your own target card**

**Keeping a conversation going:**

- 'that's interesting'
- 'then what?'
- nod in agreement

Add more ideas

# Glossary

**accent** – the aspects of *pronunciation* relating to where a person comes from, for example, *bath* with a short /a/ spoken in Yorkshire, *bath* with a long /a/ used in the South East

**alliteration** – a sequence of words which begin with the same sound or sounds, e.g. 'Colourful caterpillars climb cautiously'

**articulation** – the movements of the tongue, lips, teeth, vocal cords etc. that produce speech sounds

**attention** – the ability to knowingly focus on an activity, by listening or looking

**blends** – two or more consonants together in a spoken or written word: tr, str

**concept** – a combination of ideas, words and images which is broader than a single word, e.g. concept 'big' includes all the ideas of the words huge, enormous, older, whale, elephant, forest, universe

**conversation** – turns at talking involving a speaker and listener

**dialect** – the aspects of *grammar* and *vocabulary* relating to where a person comes from, for example 'a wee girl' in Scotland, 'a little girl' elsewhere

**discourse** – connected sentences, in speech and writing

**grammar** – the rules regarding how sentences are constructed. Made up of **syntax** [the structure], and **morphology** [how words are made]

**higher order thinking** – thinking related to evaluation and analysis

**idea** – 'any content of the mind especially the conscious mind, mental representation of something, the thought of something, concept' *Collins English Dictionary*

**inference** – connecting context clues and general knowledge in spoken or written language in order to understand

**intonation** – pitch changes used to express meaning, for example a rising intonation is used to indicate a question being asked

**learning style** – the way individuals prefer to learn, e.g., by doing (kinaesthetic), by seeing, (visual) by listening (auditory), smelling (olfactory), tasting (gustatory)

**listening** – the skill of paying attention to the information we hear

**lower order thinking** – thinking relating to knowledge and facts

**memory** – sorts and stores information and organises it for future use

- **short-term memory** – used to store a limited amount of information for a few seconds
- **working memory** – used to store one piece of information while working on another piece of the problem
- **long-term memory** – used to store information for long periods so that it can be retrieved later

**meta-cognition** – to reflect on one's own thinking; thinking about thinking.

**Mind Map™** – a way of recording and organising information using colour, single words, pictures and symbols. In a mind map the links are shown between the ideas

**morphology** – the structure of the word which includes word endings attached to the root word, which convey additional meaning: jump**ed**, quick**ly**

**phonology** – the sound system of a language

**phonological awareness** – the skill of being aware of sounds in words

**representations** – the different ways that information about words is stored in our minds. Includes: its meaning, what it sounds like, the grammar of the word, muscle movements used when saying the word, and how it looks when written

**rime** – the last vowel and consonant or consonant blend in a word or syllable: h<u>at</u>, cl<u>amp</u>

**rhythm** – the combined features of pitch, loudness, speed and silence in speech produce the rhythm of speech

**scaffolding** – building a framework around the curriculum which supports pupil's thinking to enable them to carry out the task. This can include: purposeful talk, prior knowledge, visual support, reviewing, as well as link to other learning. Takes account of all different kinds of learning

**stress** – variation of loudness of the individual syllables in a word, for example the second syllable is stressed in the word 'un<u>for</u>tunate'

**thinking** 'to exercise the mind ............. to make a decision, ponder' *Collins English Dictionary*

**vocabulary** – individual words, often referred to different parts of speech, i.e. usually relating to nouns, verbs, adjectives and adverbs

**visualisation** – turning information and ideas into pictures in the head

**word** – the smallest meaningful part of the language that can stand alone, e.g. *man, jump, sad*

**word web** – a way of showing how words are connected around a main concept

**writing frame** – a structured prompt to support writing which may include opening phrases and vocabulary

# References

Bath, J.B., Chinn, S.J., Knox, D.E., *Test of Cognitive Style in Mathematics*, Slisson

*Collins English Dictionary* (1991) Harper Collins Publishers

Crystal, D. (2003) *The Cambridge Encyclopedia of The English Language*, Cambridge University Press

Fisher, R. (1995) *Teaching Children to Learn,*. Nelson Thornes

www.nelsonthornes.com

Fisher, R. (1990) *Teaching Children to Think*, Nelson Thornes

www.nelsonthornes.com

Given, B.K. Reid, .G. (1999) *Learning Styles, A Guide for Teachers and Parents*, Red Rose Publications

Gray, C. (1994) *My Social Stories Book*, Jessica Kinglsey Publishers, London

www.jkp.com

Grunwell, P. (1982) *Clinical Phonology*, London, Croom Helm

Jordan R., Powell, S. (1995) *Understanding and Teaching Children with Autism*, Wiley

Lipman, M. (2003) *Thinking in Education*, Cambridge University Press

www.uk.cambridge.org

www.fultonpublishers.co.uk

Vygotsky, L.S. (1962) *Thought and Language*, The M.I.T. Press, Cambridge, Massachusetts

www.standards.dfes.gov.uk/thinkingskills/guidance

# Useful Resources and Suppliers

## Thinking of Ideas

*de Bono's Thinking Course*, de Bono, E. (2004), BBC Books

*Co-operative Games*. Incentive Plus, PO Box 5220, Great Horwood, Milton Keynes, MK17 0YN. Tel: 01908 526120. www.incentiveplus.co.uk

*Finish The Story*. Learning Materials Ltd., Dixon Street, Monmore Green, Wolverhampton, WV2 2BX. Tel: 01902 454026. www.learningmaterials.co.uk

Robert Fisher, *Games for Thinking*. Nash Pollock Publishing. 9 Carlton Close, Grove, Wantage, Oxfordshire OX12 0PU.

*Games for Talking: Top 5*. Winslow, Goyt Side Road, Chesterfield, Derbyshire, S40 2PH. Tel: 0845 921 1777. www.winslow-press.co.uk

*Hedbanz for Kids*. Letterbox, Tregony, Truro, TR2 5TL. Tel: 0870 600 7878. www.letterbox.co.uk

*Ideas to Go: Thinking Skills*. Taskmaster Ltd., Morris Road, Leicester LE2 6BR. Tel: 0116 270 4286. www.taskmasteronline.co.uk

*Pass the Bomb Junior*. Letterbox, Tregony, Truro, TR2 5TL. Tel: 0870 600 7878. www.letterbox.co.uk

*Thinking Out Of The Box*. Incentive Plus, PO Box 5220, Great Horwood, Milton Keynes, MK17 0YN. Tel: 01908 526120. www.incentiveplus.co.uk

## Organising Ideas

Eva Goffman, *Introducing Children to Mind Mapping*. The Anglo American Book Company Ltd., Crown Buildings, Bancyfelin, Carmarthen, Wales SA33 4ZZ. Tel: 01267 211880. www.anglo-american.co.uk.

*Super Eva*. LDA, Duke Street, Wisbech, Cambridgeshire PE13 2AE. Tel: 01945 463441. www.LDAlearning.com

*Story Starters Fun Deck*. Taskmaster Ltd., Morris Road, Leicester LE2 6BR. Tel: 0116 270 4286. www.taskmasteronline.co.uk

*Think About It*. Black Sheep Press, 67 Middleton, Cowling, Keighley, W. Yorks. BD22 0DQ. Tel: 01535 631 346. www.blacksheep-epress.com

*Write Away*. Learning Materials Ltd., Dixon Street, Monmore Green, Wolverhampton, WV2 2BX. Tel: 01902 454026. www.learningmaterials.co.uk

## Finding the Right Words

Anna Rhodes, *Rhodes to Language*. STASS Publications, 44 North Road, Ponteland, Northumberland NE20 9UR. Tel: 01661 822316. www.stasspublications.co.uk

*Compare and Contrast Fun Deck, Let's Name Fun Deck*. Taskmaster Ltd., Morris Road, Leicester LE2 6BR. Tel: 0116 270 4286. www.taskmasteronline.co.uk

*Guess What*. Chad Valley Toys, 242-246 Marylebone Road, London, NW1 6Jl. www.woolworths.co.uk.

## Speaking in Sentences

*Reversible Verbs*. Taskmaster Ltd., Morris Road, Leicester LE2 6BR. Tel: 0116 270 4286. www.taskmasteronline.co.uk

*50 Quick Play Grammar Games*. Linguisystems, Inc., East Moline, IL 61244-9700, USA. Tel: 800-776-4332. www.linguisystems.com

*Say and Do Grammar Game Boards.* Taskmaster Ltd.,
Morris Road, Leicester LE2 6BR. Tel: 0116 270 4286.
www.taskmasteronline.co.uk

*Stile Grammar and Punctuation.* LDA, Duke Street,
Wisbech, Cambridgeshire PE13 2AE. Tel: 01945 463441.
www.LDAlearning.com

## Speaking Clearly

Andrew Burnett and Jackie Wylie, *Soundaround.*
*Developing Phonological Awareness Skills in the*
*Foundation Stage.* David Fulton Publishers, London (2002).
www.fultonpublishers.co.uk

Peter J Hatcher, *Sound Linkage*, 2000, Harcourt
Assessment. www.harcourt-uk.com

*Talking Phonology.* Taskmaster Ltd., Morris Road,
Leicester LE2 6BR. Tel: 0116 270 4286.
www.taskmasteronline.co.uk

*Sentifix*, Gill Matthews, Philip and Tacey, North Way,
Andover, Hamts, SP105BA. www.philiandtacey.co.uk

## Thinking and Speaking in Conversation

*Educational Care, A System for Understanding and*
*Helping Children with Learning Problems at Home and at*
*School.* Levine, M. (1994) Educators Publishing Service, Inc.,
Cambridge Massachusetts.

*Exploring Pragmatic Language.* Harcourt Education,
Halley Court, Jordan Hill, Oxford OX2 8EJ. Tel: 01865
888188. www.harcourt-uk.com

*Oral Language.* Prim-Ed Publishing-UK, PO Box 2840,
Coventry, CV6 5ZY. Tel. 0870 876 0151. www.prim-ed.com

*Say and Do Positive Pragmatic Game Boards.* Winslow,
Goyt Side Road, Chesterfield, Derbyshire, S40 2PH. Tel:
0845 921 1777. www.winslow-press.co.uk

# Index

# Acknowledgements

The publishers would like to thank the following for permission to use their copyright material. It is the belief of both the publishers and the authors that every effort has been made to trace copyright holders. However, should there be any omissions in this respect, we apologise and on receipt of relevant information, agree to make the appropriate acknowledgements in future editions.

## Illustrations

Donald, Steve (1999) *Ghost for Sale*, © Barrington Stoke www.barringtonstoke.co.uk

Donald, Steve (2001) *Pitt Street Pirates*, © Barrington Stoke www.barringtonstoke.co.uk

## Texts

Dodd, Lynley. (1990.) *Slinky Malinki*, First published in New Zealand © Mallinson Rendell Publishers Ltd., Wellington.

Deary, Terry (1999) *Ghost for Sale*, © Barrington Stoke www.barringtonstoke.co.uk

Crystal, D. (2003) *The Cambridge Encyclopedia of The English Language*, © Cambridge University Press

Fisher, R. (1995) *Teaching Children to Learn*, © Nelson Thornes, 1995. www.nelsonthornes.com

Jordan, R., Powell, S. (1995) *Understanding and Teaching Children with Autism*, © John Wiley & Sons Ltd.

Vygotsky, L.S. (1986) *Thought and Language*, © The M.I.T. Press, Cambridge, Massachusetts